BRISTOL

Discovering Bristol on Foot

Compiled by Peter Gould
Maps by Neil Burlton
Photographs by Denzil Ellis ARPS DPAGB

The Ramblers

BRISTOL · CITY · COUNCIL

THE RAMBLERS · BRISTOL GROUP ⇒ MOVING FORWARD

Whilst every effort has been made to check these routes, mistakes do happen and the city is subject to changes, so neither the authors nor the Ramblers' Association can accept responsibility for any inconvenience they may cause. To correct mistakes, or indeed to suggest improvements or new walks for a second edition, write to 18 Hampton Park, Bristol, BS6 6LH or e-mail bristolbacks@aol.com.

Neither the Ramblers' Association nor the City Council necessarily endorse the opinions expressed by the writers.

The Ramblers' Association is a charity (306089) set up in 1935 with the aims of promoting rambling, protecting rights of way, campaigning for access to open countryside and defending the beauty of the countryside.

Nationally, the Association acts as a pressure group, lobbying Ministers about issues of concern to walkers, commenting on official reports and proposed new legislation, giving advice to official committees and briefing sympathetic M.P.s and peers. Its Areas play a similar role in respect of Highway Authorities and other units of local government. Over 400 local groups organise walks and carry out footpath work.

For further information, contact:
The Ramblers' Association, 2nd Floor, Camelford House,
87-90 Albert Embankment, London, SE1 7TW
☎ 020 7339 8500
e-mail: ramblers@londonramblers.org.uk
web: www.ramblers.org.uk
Bristol Group: www.bristolramblers.freeserve.co.uk

ISBN 1-901184-52-8

© Maps & text Ramblers' Association 2002
Photographs Denzil Ellis 2002

FOREWORD

B RISTOL has a wealth of interesting places to offer the walker who explores the highways and, more especially, the back ways of the city, with time to stand and stare.

Whether in the city centre or further out, the squares and bridges, churches and pubs are landmarks in our history. This book opens our eyes to the past and present. Names in everyday use can suddenly have new significance such as my recent discovery that Oliver Cromwell actually stayed at a farm near the top of Cromwell Road, or just be fun such as 'There and Back Again Lane', for a city centre cul-de-sac.

Turn through an archway, up a flight of steps or along a narrow passage in Bristol and, so often there is a discovery to be made. Tailor's Court is a good example, just off Broad Street, or the steps at the bottom of Jacob's Wells Road leading to Brandon Hill Park. A favourite lane of mine is Johnny Ball Lane leading off Lewins Mead, but who was he and why a lane in his name?

The Ramblers' Association in Bristol is to be congratulated for offering us this excellent reason for city walking and, should we become engrossed and take longer than intended, for offering an alternative way back by bus or ferry.

If you are interested in the history of the city, enjoying a quiet garden, seeing sculpture old and new, or just finding a shortcut to avoid the traffic, this book is a good companion.

I promise you will not go far before stopping to appreciate something that you have not noticed before. Walking is the best way to see the city, this book will add to your enjoyment.

Val Davey M.P.

SYMBOLS USED ON THE MAPS

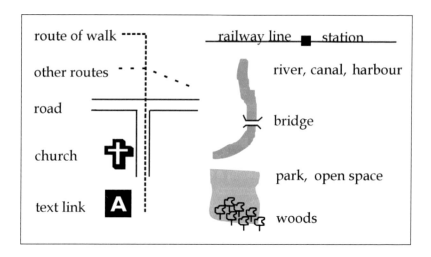

route of walk

other routes

road

church

text link

railway line ■ station

river, canal, harbour

bridge

park, open space

woods

Even though these walks are within the city, suitable footwear and a waterproof are still advised. All the walks are accessible by public transport. Check the times of buses, especially on infrequent routes, and trains. We have done our best to provide accurate and up to date information, but services are liable to alteration at short notice.

THE BRISTOL TRIANGLE
A LONG DISTANCE CITY WALK

This 18 mile city walk was devised in 2001 by members of the Bristol Group of the Ramblers' Association with funding and assistance from Bristol City Council. Offering wonderful views within and across the city, the Triangle brings the rambler, occasional walker or beginner to explore the Waterfront, Durdham Down, Ashton Court and Blaise Estate as well as the heart and history of the city. A leaflet describing the route is available from the Tourist Information Centre.

CONTENTS

INTRODUCTION

T HE VISITOR TO BRISTOL TODAY will find a busy, vibrant and developing city with some of the finest cityscapes and buildings in Europe. Its unique geographical features, with the River Avon's easy access to the sea and the confluence of the rivers Frome and Trym, have determined both its development and prestigious history.

These natural features encouraged and supported both the early development of world-wide trading links and through the centuries the establishment of many different industries in Bristol.

In more recent times the dramatic Avon Gorge has attracted tourists. In the nineteenth century the young Brunel demonstrated his extraordinary engineering expertise when he won a competition for the design of a suspension bridge to cross the Gorge. Further evidence of the impact of Brunel's vision and engineering ability is to be found across Bristol.

Bristol's origins are Anglo-Saxon. By the 900s AD there is evidence of a busy and thriving town based where Bristol Bridge is positioned today. Domesday book entries confirm Bristol as a prosperous trading centre. King John's Charter of 1188 shows Bristol to be a growing merchants town exporting wool, cloth, ropes and lead and importing wine from France, Spain and Portugal.

In 1239-47, during the reign of Henry III, a new and improved harbour was built by diverting the course of the River Frome. There have been many subsequent changes to the river routes, the harbours and the docks of Bristol. Today, many of these areas are turned over to attractive waterside residential developments.

Up to the end of the fourteenth century Bristol was the greatest wool exporting town in England. For centuries she was the nation's second port and, during the eighteenth century, its second largest city.

During the fifteenth century the sailors and navigators of Bristol more than played their part in the discovery of the new world. It was from Bristol that John Cabot sailed on his 'accidental' discovery of North America. Today a replica of the *Matthew*, Cabot's ship, rests in the Bristol harbour.

Through the centuries new industries such as sugar refining developed and trade continued to grow. In the eighteenth and nineteenth centuries, trade in slaves, sugar and tobacco contributed to the prosperity of the city. The dramatic and extensive Georgian terraces of the Clifton area of the city reflect the wealth of the merchants of those times.

It used to be said that wherever you stood and in whatever direction you looked in Bristol you would be able to see at least one church spire. With recent building developments this may not now hold true. Nevertheless, the architectural legacy of Bristol's religious past is still very evident, despite the disastrous effects of Henry VIII's dissolution of the monasteries and the equally damaging effects of the German Blitz during the Second World War.

The visitor to Bristol may wonder where the term 'backs' comes from. There are three theories. The least likely derivation is from an Old English word 'bak' meaning river. This is unconvincing because 'bak' is not recorded in Anglo-Saxon literature. A more likely theory is that it comes from the French 'bac' meaning ferry. Often it seems to be a synonym for Quay, as in Welsh Back or Redcliffe Back, which are streets near the water. But there are also Backs away from the water, such as Back Road in Southville. Other Backs have been lost in development like Little James Back at the bottom of Pithay, or they have been renamed. The most likely theory is that a 'Back' is a street lying behind another street like Temple Back behind Temple Street.

Bristol Backs is a walker's guide to the city including areas many tourists may not usually visit. For those interested in finding out more historical context and detail, the standard work is Bryan Little's *Bristol* supplemented by the Historical Association's pamphlets and Bristol Industrial Archaeological Society's publications. Gomme, Jenner and Little's *Bristol, an Architectural History* and the Royal West of England Academy's pamphlet, *The Bristol Sculpture Guide*, provide further information about public art and architecture. Recently published, Veronica Smith's *The Street Names of Bristol* is a suggestive though not an infallible study. Like any book touching on the History of Bristol, this one draws heavily on John Latimer's *Annals of Bristol* and also on Joseph Leech's *Bristol Churchgoer*. Details of other sources on request.

The Bristol Group of the Ramblers' Association wishes to thank everybody involved in the production of the book. The names of the designers of the walks are recorded on the contents page; you may note a difference in style from one chapter to another. Other Ramblers have checked the walks, read the text, designed, advised and administered: Nigel Andrews, Don Baillie, Margaret Blake, Barbara Edwards, Jim Grant, Jill Hathaway, Peregrine Howell, Patsy Hudson, Maureen Johnson, Mary Magro, Geoff Mullett, Jean Oliver, Caroline Poole, Sandy Riley, Marietta Starbuck, Caroline Theyer, Marge Thomas, Nick Wilkes, Geoff Yorath. Bristol Group acknowledges assistance given by the staff of Bristol City Library and officers of Bristol City Council. This book would not have been possible without the financial assistance of the City Council.

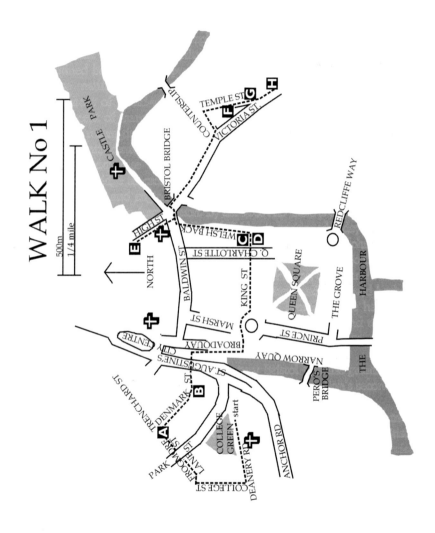

WALK No 1

HISTORIC PUB TRAIL

Description: *A short trail designed to give you a reasonable length of time to visit each inn.*
Length: *2 miles.*
Refreshments: *Besides the pubs themselves, there are many cafés en route.*
Transport: *Many buses serve College Green. Nos 1, 54 and 55 link the beginning and end of the walk.*

The starting point is College Green in the centre of the city. Walking behind the Council House, turn right into Frog Lane and pass under Park Street, along Frogmore Street to the first port of call, the Hatchet Inn.

This inn **A**, structurally Bristol's oldest, was originally in Frog Lane even before Park Street (so named because of Bullock Park) was built. The lane was of great importance, being the chief way of driving to Clifton when it was an isolated village. The pub is a Grade II* listed building which won a Civic Trust award for its renovation in 1969. The timber work dates from the sixteenth century. Its name the Hatchet may derive from tree felling. A fine seventeenth century ceiling can be found on the first floor which extends the whole length of the front. The beam that spans the room and carries the floor over is 22 feet in length. The inn was noted for its history of sportsmen and a boxing ring was set up at the rear for bare knuckle prize fighting. Hanham's Thomas Crib was a regular visitor during the 1850s. Rat catching and cock fighting were also once popular entertainments.

Kenny Baker of 'Star Wars' fame has twisted the night away on the public bar.

Continue along Denmark Avenue into Denmark Street.

The Bunch of Grapes **B**, circa 1700, is known as a theatre pub. A typical city pub, it contains an L-shaped interior with one long bar and serves a good selection of real ales.

Of equal interest are the huge range of theatre posters, covering every wall and showing the many artistes who have walked through the Hippodrome stage door on the opposite side of the street. Note the sign.

Turn right and cross the City Centre at the end of Broad Quay, by the pelican crossings, heading towards the roundabout at this corner of Queen Square. Turn left off the roundabout into King Street for the Naval Volunteer (the Volly). Here also was the King William Tavern, with its original entrance in King William Avenue.

At the far end of King Street **C** is the Old Duke, a celebrated jazz pub since the late 1950s. (The original Duke was possibly Wellington rather than Ellington.) On entering, take a long look at all the old jazz posters that adorn the ceiling and the photos on the walls. Many stars such as Kenny Baker, Orange Kellin and Monty Sunshine have performed here.

Opposite the Duke is the Llandoger Trow **D** dating from 1664. It is named after the flat bottomed barges that used to trade across the Severn berth in Welsh Back. 'Llandoger' is derived from the name of the village 'Llandogo' on the River Wye.

The pub was converted from five seventeenth century houses. Only three remain; the two on the left hand side were blitzed. The site is being redeveloped. The half-timbered front is one of the most notable in the city. The original entrance door (similar to the one at the Hatchet) is now in a passageway. The remains of seventeenth century woodwork on the ground floor facing King Street indicate the nature of the character imparted to this row of gabled houses. Originally the Llandoger had some projections on the return to Queen Charlotte Street. It is one of the few inns retaining its ironwork over the pavement for supporting a lamp. The building still contains the original back stairs. Local folklore recalls the ceiling over the public bar being coloured with outlines of the female form. The lady licensee of that period became concerned by the seamen sitting drinking their ale, their gaze permanently aloft. She soon had it painted all over in black.

This inn is alleged to have served as a model for the Admiral Benbow in Robert Louis Stevenson's *Treasure Island*. A far better bet would appear to be the Hole in the Wall, nearby in the Grove. This pub really does have a spy glass in the front of the building.

The Llandoger has another literary association. Here, it is said, Daniel Defoe met Alexander Selkirk, the real life Robinson Crusoe, who had been marooned on one Bristol-backed privateering cruise, led by William Dampier, and rescued by another, led by Woodes Rogers. The captain of the ship that picked up Selkirk was Thomas Dover, the physician to St Peter's Hospital, remembered medically for centuries for his powder, a lucratively addictive blend of opium and ipecacuanha, sedative, emetic and sudorific which seems to have been tried for almost anything. The Italian army was still using it during World War II.

(In *A Tour through the Whole Island of Great Britain*, Defoe remarked 'the greatest inconveniences of Bristol, are its situation, and the tenacious folly of its inhabitants'. Apart from that, he rather admired the place.)

Turn left along Welsh Back and right into Baldwin Street to Bristol Bridge. Turn left and cross Baldwin Street by the pelican crossing, into High Street. A little way up, on the left hand side is the Rummer, which has been closed for years.

The Rummer **E** is shut at present for another of the refurbishments in its long history. In 1241, the Green Lattis occupied the site. A lattice was a customary feature of an alehouse; usually, however, they were red. It was succeeded by the Abyndon. Later it was known as the Jonas. About 1565 the premises were again renamed, the New Inn or the New Star. John Wood of Bath set back and rebuilt the Rummer. In Matthews Guide to Bristol, there is an interesting list of mail coaches to London, Wales and Birmingham, all of which started from the Rummer tavern. From here, Coleridge edited his radical paper, *The Watchman*.

Inside was displayed an ample wood and copper 'rummer', explained as a drinking mug for rum. The words are probably not closely connected. 'Rummer' is a word of Flemish origin, possibly meaning 'Roman' glass. The large drinking glasses called rummers were associated not with molasses based spirits but with Rhenish wine, hock.

'Rum' is a shortened form, perhaps, of the fanciful 'rumbullion' or 'rumbustion'. It may, or may not, have to do with the early seventeenth century canting term 'rum', meaning 'excellent'. 'Rum booze' certainly referred to good drink of any sort, including Canary. Ultimately, a memory of imperial splendour, conjecture derives this word too from 'Rome'. As Middleton's Roaring Girle, a transvestite highwayman sang:

A gage of ben rom bouse
In a bousing ken of Rom-vile,
Is benar than a caster,
Peck, pennam, lay or popler
Which we mill in deuse a vile
I wud couch till a palliard docked my dell
So my bousy nab might skew rom-bouse well

(A quart of good city drink in a London pub is better than any food or clothes we could nick in the country. I'd lie quiet while a dosser screwed my girl if I could have a proper drink.)

Return to Bristol Bridge, cross it into Victoria Street, and immediately after Redcliff Street cross the road by the zebra crossing. Turn left into Counterslip. Turn first right into Temple Street for the Cornubia **F**. *Further on, on the left, is the King's Head.*

170 years ago this thoroughfare possessed at least 18 taverns and inns. 'Cornubia' is the Latinised form of 'Cornwall'. There were strong links between Bristol and Cornwall, founded on trade, especially the supply of copper ore to the brass industry. (The son of William Borlase, the Cornish antiquary was an apothecary at the Infirmary.)

The paddle steamer *Cornubia*, which gave its name to public houses in Bristol and Hayle, was launched in 1858 for the Hayle and Bristol Steam Packet Company. She was a frequent visitor to Bristol when the Cornubia Tavern was built in 1860. London speculators bought her to run the blockade in the American Civil War 1861-65. She was renamed *Lady Davis* and in 1863 made 22 successful runs before being captured off New Inlet North Carolina. She was resold and re-registered as a merchant vessel under the name of *New England*. In 1871 she was converted to a sailing barquette of 462 tons by Gibson & Baxter of Boston, Massachusetts.

This remains a quiet, pleasant pub with a marvellous selection of real ales and also perry (pear cider). It was awarded pub of the year by Bristol & District branch of CAMRA in 2001. Note the 'lambs tongue' windows, the left one being the door.

The King's Head  has been in existence over 150 years, but it was probably not erected for the purpose it now serves. The ground floor occupies an eighteenth century building which once displayed the original brickwork. At first floor level there was a projecting lamp, so familiar on inns at that time. In Temple Street almost every trade was represented. Glassmakers, cutters and engravers resided here. Carpenters, joiners, vinegar and pipe makers, a school mistress and a pencil maker are but a few who lived in the neighbourhood.

The inn retains its original bar and ornamental fittings and also displays on the interior wall a case containing a Charles II crown piece of 1673.

Come out into Victoria Street and turn left. Last but not least of all these inns is the Shakespeare (1636) **H**.

Apart from some alterations that have taken place, this old house, which is so well known, retains an atmosphere of the past and is a notable addition to the seventeenth century architecture of Bristol. The name of Dick Turpin has been associated with it upon his visits to Bristol, but this has never been substantiated.

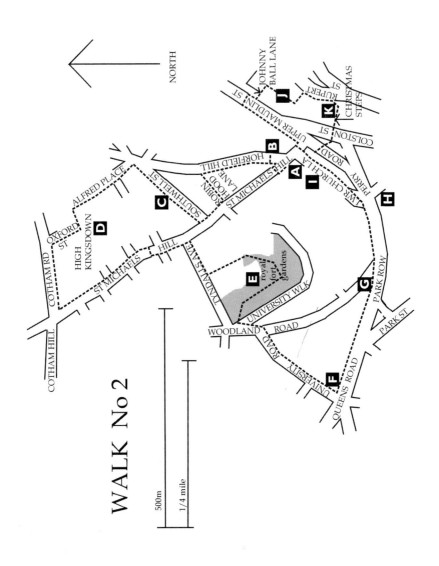

PLAQUES OF CENTRAL BRISTOL

Description: *A short but steep walk taking in the new 'blue plaques' near the centre.*
Length: *2 miles.*
Refreshments: *Pubs and cafés en route.*
Transport: *Buses to Centre.*

St Michael's Church **A** is mostly Georgian with a fifteenth century tower. The church having been redundant for three years, is shortly to be developed by an IT firm called Coolcrypt.

From the west door of St Michael's Church, go to St Michael's Hill and cross to Horfield Road.

Most houses date from sixteenth and seventeenth centuries. Nearly all are listed. The bottom stand of four are timber framed and built in 1637 by a family from Axbridge.

George Pocock, who lived near the church, experimented with kites to power boats and carriages. In a good wind, a tricycle carrying four people could reach twenty five miles an hour. Better still, it was exempt from turnpike tolls. A schoolmaster, Pocock also designed a flogging machine. Surely he deserves a plaque with a citation for green transport and old-fashioned values.

Note the plaque to Sir Michael Redgrave **B**, born in theatrical digs at No 4 and named after the Church.

Sir Michael Redgrave
1908 - 1985

Film star and actor
was born here

Bengough's almshouses were built in 1818. (Bengough was unlucky. On his last day in office as Lord Mayor in 1793, at a demonstration against the toll on Bristol Bridge, the Hereford Militia whose assistance he had enlisted without regard for proper procedure, shot and killed an innocent bystander. Bengough's last official acts were attempts to regularise the use of troops in retrospect and to rig the inquest. Under his successor, 14 more rioters were killed.)

Turn left up steps into Robin Hood Lane. Go right past St Michael's Hospital and right into Southwell Street.

The University Veterinary College **C** occupies an Edwardian school building. The Bristol School Board had previously had a special school for truants on the site, subjecting them to two hours military style drill a day.

Turn left into Alfred Place - note colourful display of late seventeenth century houses. At the end go left into High Kingsdown and right into Oxford Street to emerge in Cotham Road. Turn left to Cotham Parish Church.

Above eyelevel on the last house in Alfred Place, backing on Montague Place, a small sculpture depicts a few of the workers on the restoration project.

High Kingsdown **D** was a prize winning 1974 housing scheme, attempting to combine high density, low rise and privacy. The Kings Arms, a Victorian pub was refurbished for its 'village green'. Note plaque on the outside wall of the church, denoting the boundary stone of the mediaeval City of Bristol. It was rescued and repositioned when the chapel was built. The gallows stood here on the dusty track leading into the city. (See Walk no 8.) Note the Arts and Crafts movement Western College and the Homeopathic Hospital by Oatley. Just down Cotham Hill, Cotham House on the left, with a frieze of Cotham Landscape Marble, was the home of George White who ran the tram system and founded the Bristol Aeroplane Company.

Turn left into St Michael's Hill and after 200 yards turn right into Tyndall Avenue, and left under arch of the Physics Block of the University into Royal Fort Gardens **E**.

The Corporation began to fortify the city in 1642, nevertheless it was captured by Prince Rupert in 1643. The Royalists reinforced the Windmill Hill Fort which was used as Rupert's headquarters and renamed Royal Fort. The City was recaptured in 1645 and the fort strengthened again. The defences were built by conscript labour and paid for by local taxation and forced loans. After the Parliamentary victory, in 1655, Cromwell made the citizens of Bristol meet the cost of destroying the works. Of the Royal Fort, only the gate house remains.

Exit into Woodland Road and cross to University Road, walking down past the Grammar School and left into Queen's Road.

Note the Bristol Byzantine façade of Brown's Restaurant **F**, formerly the City Museum, then the University Refectory. Read the plaque on the wall of the present Museum and Art Gallery dedicated to Colonel Henry Washington - an ancestor of George Washington. Many skirmishes were fought along this road during the Civil War.

Pass the Wills Tower with its fine views down Park Street and stop by the University Engineering Building.

Oatley's Wills Tower was not erected until after the First World War, which must make it the last public building in its style. The construction, however, was modern steel frame. Note façade of a cinema incorporated into the building and read the plaque to Nipper the HMV dog **G**. Opposite, by the garage, is a plaque to remind us that the Princes Theatre stood there. Opened in 1867, as the New Theatre, it seated 2,400. Two years, later a disastrous crush on Boxing Day, killing fourteen people, had a calamitous effect on the theatre's fortunes until its name was changed.

Famous for its pantomime, which Bernard Shaw praised, the Princes, not the Royal, was Bristol's principle theatre until it was destroyed in the Second World War.

Note the fine fin de siècle loos on the corner of Woodland and Park Row.

Proceed along Park Row and where this becomes Perry Road, turn left up Lower Church Lane.

The Elizabethan Red Lodge ▉ on the right was built as a retreat for the family who lived in a much grander house on the site of the Colston Hall. The Red Lodge has stunning panelling and a restored knot garden. Note plaques on the front of the building.

On the left of Lower Church Lane is a fine Victorian school. The Old Rectory is partly built in Strawberry Hill Gothic ▉.

Cross at lights, go left down Upper Maudlin Street, with the newly completed Children's Hospital on the left. Here, cross the road at the lights, find Johnny Ball Lane ▉ unsigned and slightly to your right beside Jameson's Restaurant and wander down. Then turn right.

Note the St James' Parish Boundary stone eight foot up the right-hand wall and at the bottom the restored sugar refinery, now the Hotel du Vin. (For a fuller gruesome account of the lane, see Walk no 4.)

Note the fine statue of a horseman by David Backhouse and the twelfth century St Bartholomew's Cloister. (See Walk no 22.)

Climb Christmas Steps to the right.

A plaque ▉ on the wall to the right commemorates Colonel Lunsford, a Royalist shot through the heart when Prince Rupert took the city. (For a while, the street was known as Lunsford's Steps.) An inscription above the alms gatherers' niche at the top of the steps, commemorates the 'steppering down' of the street. Foster's Almshouses, with the Chapel of the Three Kings of Cologne are built in Burgundian style and are in direct contrast with the tram sheds opposite, built in 1888 to provide a horse drawn tram service to Clifton. The tram sheds are shortly to be renovated to provide a restaurant.

Go up the steep Bristol Steps, cross Perry Road and return to St Michael's churchyard.

Refresh yourself at the Scotchman and his Pack. One explanation of the name derives it from a 'scotch', a portable brake which the scotchman applied to carts descending the hill to prevent them getting out of control. Sometimes the scotch glowed red from the friction created. Another more plausible theory is that the pub, at one of the main entrances to the city, tried to attract the custom of pedlars.

Traditionally, Scots, besides living on oatmeal and suffering from the itch, made their living as itinerant tradesman, carrying their wares in packs.

A walk that touches on a mass of history - perhaps to be explored again and in more depth.

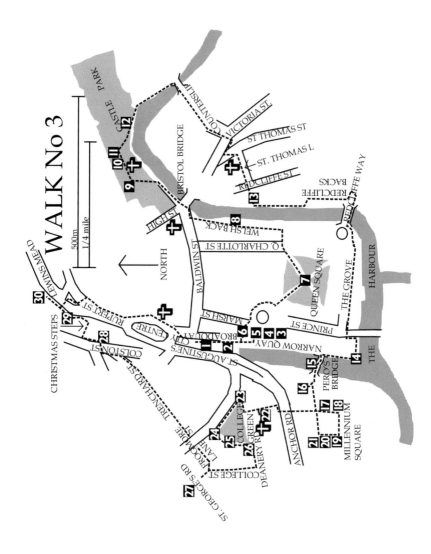

SCULPTURE TRAIL

Description: *This walk gives a fascinating tour of some 30 public statues and sculptures, many of them hidden from public gaze. The walk starts on the City Centre through Queen Square to Castle Park, along the harbour to Millennium Square and on to College Green returning to the City Centre.*

Length: *approx. 2½ miles (4 kms).*

Refreshments: *Numerous cafés and pubs on route.*

Transport: *Buses to City Centre.*

The walk starts at the Statue of Neptune **1** on the City Centre. This originally stood at the head of St Augustine's Reach on the Harbourside but was resited in 1999. Cast by the Bristol founder John Rendall in 1723. Originally conceived as an ornamental flourish to a new water supply in Temple Street, the figure, standing on the back of a dolphin, looks suitably hoary-bearded and patriarchal, although the plump sleekness of his pot-belly suggests the laxity of a voluptuary rather than the moody energy of the sea king.

Walk towards the harbour, noting the five plaques adjoining the five seats on the right hand side of the City Centre walkway.

2a Replica of the plaque at Bristol Basin, New York, which commemorates the Bristol bomb rubble, used as ships' ballast to cross the Atlantic, finally used as landfill to form the basin.

2b Samuel Plimsoll, M.P. for Derby, originator of the load line known as the Plimsoll Line on ships, born at 9, Colston Avenue 1824, died 1898. Strangely, in his native city the seaman's canvas shoe also named after him is called a 'dap' instead.

2c John Cabot and son Sebastian Cabot sailing from Bristol on the *Matthew* to discover America in 1497.

2d Centenary of 100 years of the Port of Bristol Authority 1848-1948.

2e Replica plaque of town trail named in honour of John Cabot who landed in Cape Cod, Nova Scotia, Canada on 24th June 1497.

Cross City Centre to Narrow Quay, to the courtyard on the waterfront side of Broad Quay House.

The Apotheosis of Sabrina **3** by Gerald Laing (1981). The dramatic goddess of the River Severn and her youthful supporters are almost hidden from public view!

Walk around to the front of Broad Quay House.

Look through the glazed entrance to view **4** The Pigeons by Thomas Hill (1998) hanging from the foyer ceiling. On the building at first floor level are **5** 15 Ceramic Panels (1980) by Phillippa Threlfall and Kennedy Collings which depicts the industry and commerce of Bristol.

Cross Broad Quay to the statue at the end of Marsh Street.

6 Isambard Kingdom Brunel by John Doubleday (1982).

Continue past roundabout and into the centre of Queen Square.

7 The statue of William III by John Michael Rysbrack (1736), a splendid equestrian statue of the King in Roman heroic style uniform which originally cost the Bristol Whigs some £17,500, a small fortune in 1736!

Turn left to the corner of Queens Square cross Queen Charlotte Street and follow Queen Square Avenue to Welsh Back. Turn left.

8 The Merchant Seaman's Memorial (2001) commemorates the many seamen's lives lost at sea in war and in peace.

At the end of the Back, turn right and cross the approach to Bristol Bridge into Castle Park. Take diagonal path towards Wine Street and go under the footbridge, left.

9 Line from Within (1993) by Ann Christopher is an upright steel structure with a vertical slot.

Continue along left hand side of St Peter's Church

10 Throne (1993) by Rachel Fenner, a stone sculpture, which invites self-coronation.

11 Beside the Still Waters (1993) by Peter Randell-Page, tranquil linear ponds with stone pineapple shaped water fountains at each end.

Turn right to a group of silver birch trees and plaques which commemorate the 50th anniversary of the D-Day landing in Normandy in 1944. On your left is Fish.

12 Fish (1993) by Kate Malone a very attractive bronze cast drinking fountain. It echoes several themes in Bristol's past. A stylised chunk of Bristol Castle marks the history of its site. A boat records the link with the sea and the fish spouting water remind drinkers how the hunt for cod led to Bristolians discovering the new world.

Follow the harbourside walkway, over the footbridge to the road bridge. Up the steps, turn right across bridge along Counterslip. Cross Victoria Street, right, then first left into St Thomas Street. and first right into Thomas Lane. Cross Redcliffe Street to harbourside.

13 Exploration (1991) by Phillippa Threlfall, Kennedy Collings and James Blunt. In the sixteenth century, Martin Frobisher brought back from an exploratory voyage an Eskimo family which entertained the crowd by hunting duck in a kayak on the Back.

Turn left and continue along harbourside walkway past the 'blue helter-skelter' architectural feature. When you can follow the waterfront no further, follow the same line along Redcliffe Backs to Redcliffe Way. Cross road and turn right over bridge, turn left into The Grove, left at Prince Street. Right to Narrow Quay.

14 John Cabot (1985) by Stephen Joyce. This bronze statue set in the cobbles commemorates when he came to Bristol from Venice in 1495 and left Bristol to discover Newfoundland.

Turn right and continue along Narrow Quay to cross ...

15 Pero's Bridge (1998) by Eillis O'Connell is named after an African slave servant who lived and died in eighteenth century Bristol.

Walk through to New World Square.

16 Beetle sculpture (2000) by Nicola Hicks.

Continue into Millennium Square and go clockwise.

17 Water Sculpture (2000) by William Pye is a continuous flowing water feature with stainless steel columns and pools of water cascading into each other.

18 Dogs playing in pool (2000).

19 William Tyndale (2000) by Lawrence Holoscener.

20 Thomas Chatterton (2000) also by Lawrence Holoscener.

21 The statue of Cary Grant [2] by Graham Ibbeson (2001). The Hollywood film star was born in Bristol in 1904 as Archibald Leech in Hughenden Road, Horfield. He was expelled at the age of fourteen from Fairfield School, Montpelier. The statue was unveiled by his widow on the 7th December 2001, exactly 70 years from when he changed his name to Cary Grant.

Leave Square under Explore @ Bristol building adjoining the Tourist Information Office. Cross Anchor Road and up steps to the right.

22 Refugee (1980) by Norma Blake, viewed on left hand side, through gate into the Cathedral Garden.

Continue to College Green and go round anticlockwise.

23 Queen Victoria (1888) by Sir Joseph Edgar Boehm to commemorate the fiftieth year of her reign.

24 Bristol Unicorns (1950) by David McFall on the roof of the Council House.

25 John Cabot (1956) by Sir Charles Wheeler in the centre of the Council House.

26 Raja Rammohun Roy (1997) by Niranjan Pradhan.

Leave College Green by Deanery Road. Right into College Street (noting plaque to William Friese-Green on the back wall of the Council House) to cross St George's Road through gateway on right hand side of Brunel House to rear courtyard.

27 Horse and Man (1984) in resin and bronze by Stephen Joyce, which evokes the site of a nineteenth century Bristol horse market.

Continue behind the Council House along Frog Lane, under the bridge and up Frogmore Street and Trenchard Street. Cross Colston street.

28 Three Kings of Cologne (1967) by Ernest Pascoe in the early sixteenth century niches of the Chapel adjoining Fosters Almshouses.

Right down the steep Christmas Steps, left to Rupert Street.

29 Cloaked Horseman (1984) by David Backhouse.

Continue along to Lewin's Mead, on the left, the entrance to Greyfriars Offices.

30 St Francis of Assisi (1972) by Judith Bluck. Six very large bronze reliefs tell the story of St Francis.

Take the crossing behind you to the Lewins Mead traffic island where there is a statue of Samuel Morley. Two other eminent men with Bristol connections, Edmund Burke and Edward Colston, have statues on the Centre.

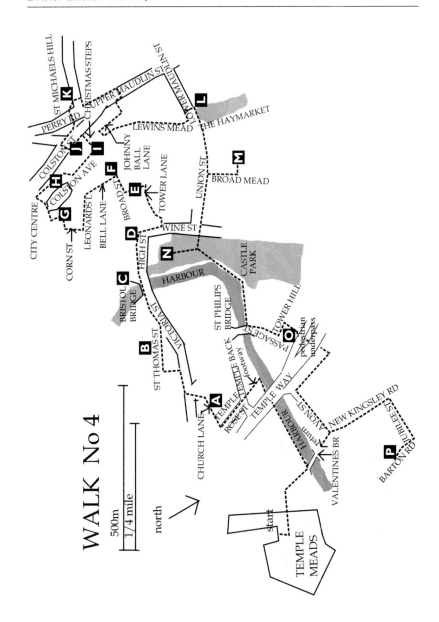

WALK No 4

500m
1/4 mile

north

TOWERS AND TRANSEPTS

Description: Bristol has always been described as a city of pubs and
churches. This time we turn our attention to some of the
churches on a walk which will give you a chance to visit a few
and look inside. If you wish to do this, make your visit during
the day between 11.00am and 4.00pm.

Length: ⅔ miles.

Refreshments: Cafés and pubs en route.

Transport: Trains and buses to Temple Meads station. Ferry.

Exit through the north side car park of Temple Meads station, following the green
pathway signs. Immediately before Valentines Bridge, turn left and pass under
Temple Bridge. Turn left into Temple Back and right into Temple Rose Street,
passing the rear of the City Inn on the left. Before Church Lane, turn right
through the churchyard to arrive at Temple Church.

This church **A** was founded in 1147 by the Knights Templar, an exclusive
and aristocratic order of chivalry. The war-damaged remains of the present
church date from 1390. The 114 foot tower leans alarmingly. (After the air
raid, an over zealous army officer wanted to pull it down as a hazard.)
There is an old story of a parishioner who used the cracks, which opened
and closed in the tower when the bells were rung, to crack walnuts.

Exit into Church Lane and fork right. Turn right into Victoria Street. Cross the
road and turn left into St Thomas Street. Next to the Fleece and Firkin, once a
brewery, is St Thomas Church.

St Thomas' Church **B** is still consecrated, but no longer used. It is open
to the public most Mondays between 11.00am and 4.00pm, accessible via
the alley between the church and the Seven Stars. Behind the altar are
paintings of Jesus preaching and the Last Supper. Handel performed here.
The north west tower dates from the original building, dedicated about
1200 to the recently martyred Thomas à Becket.

In the alley next to the church is a plaque on the Seven Stars to Revd Thomas Clarkson who stayed there whilst collecting information against the slave trade. The landlord, sympathetic to the cause, escorted him round the dock-side crimping dens.

Return to St Thomas Street. Fork left into Victoria Street, continuing on across Bristol Bridge. On the corner with Baldwin Street is St Nicholas.

St Nicholas ◪ was rebuilt 1763-69. Sections of the old 15 foot thick city wall are built into the crypt which is now a brass-rubbing centre. The Churchgoer, a Pickwickian persona of the nineteenth century journalist Joseph Leech, proprietor of the Tory *Bristol Times*, thought it the greatest incongruity, having two classes of Gothic and a Grecian interior. Pleasing, he found it, light and not inelegant, but were he a rich parishioner would be tempted to pull down the ceiling 'with its little groups of pursy seraphim and plaister of Paris clouds'. This fantasy did not survive the war. Note the church clock: unusual in that it has a second hand.

Here is buried Alderman Whitson, founder of the Red Maids School of whom his godson, John Aubrey recounted the anecdote about the foundation of his fortune which 'will last perhaps as long as Bristol is a City'. 'He was a handsome young fellow; and his old Master being dead, his Mistress one day called him into the Wine-cellar and bad him broach the best Butt in the Cellar for her; and truly he broach't his Mistrisse, who after maried him.'

At the top left of High Street, turn left into Corn Street. Before St Nicholas Market, on the left, is All Saints'. On the corner of High Street and Wine Street is Christchurch.

All Saints' **D**, a Norman foundation with a perpendicular east end and a regency cupola, is still in use, not as a parish church but as a centre for religious and urban studies.

The magnificent Christchurch was erected between 1786 and 1790. The first hallmark to catch the eye is the quarter jacks on the outside, striking the bells with their axes each quarter hour. Inside, even more splendid, is the gold and white Georgian chancel screen and elaborate ceiling.

In the mid-nineteenth century, one other church in the group, St Werburgh's, was taken away and reconstructed in the part of Bristol that bears its name. Another neighbouring church, St Ewan in Broad Street, was combined with Christchurch in the nineteenth century. When the building was demolished a perfectly preserved unembalmed corpse was found. 'To render the illustrious dead still more proof against decomposition' a group of antiquarians passed it into the oven of the Institution at Park Street. 'The oven having been unfortunately overheated the body was baked and the antiquarians to their deep chagrin, were compelled to commit once more to their mother earth the somewhat highly-savoured over-dressed proportion of the ancient alderman.'

Perhaps the most important event in religious history to take place in Broad Street was a meeting, not in any of the churches, but in the White Lion on the site of the Grand Hotel. In 1850, 300 clergymen of the Bristol Church Union, 'mother of the Church Union System', deliberated whether followers of the Oxford Movement should make an anti-Roman declaration to affirm their loyalty to the Church of England. Keble and Pusey spoke against and carried the day. A larger meeting in London followed the Bristol lead giving impetus to the ecumenical trend.

Walk along the Wine Street side of Christchurch and turn left into the Pithay, then left into Tower Lane. On your left, six foot up the wall, two carved stones mark the boundary of two parishes. Before the four-way split, turn left, passing under Fitzhardinge House. Pass St John's Cemetery to the right and go into Tailors Court.

Once through the passage way, on the left, **E** is a shell-hooded doorway with another one further on to your right opposite Horts. The latter one is over the door of the Guild Hall of Merchant Taylors and contains a colourful coat of arms.

Continue on and turn right into Broad Street. Go down to the church of St John and St John's arch standing between Bell Lane and Tower Lane.

The Church **F** is built into the old city wall. Known for its simplicity, St John's went on using a pitch pipe when all the other churches had bought organs.

Do not go under the arch, but turn left along Bell Lane. Cross Small Street and, directly opposite, go under an archway between Black Horse Personal Finance and Haptons. This is Leonard Lane. At the exit go right into Corn Street and right again into St Stephen's Street. On the left is St Stephen's Church.

St Stephen's **G** was known as the seamen's church, stemming from the time when the church was on the quayside and the old sailing ships moored in the heart of the city centre. The story that Edward Blanket, whose memorial is in the church, gave his name to the bed covering is implausible; the word is recorded before the church was built. The Churchgoer has an anecdote of plying a dozy member of the congregation with snuff to keep him awake.

From St Stephen's Church cross the Centre to St Mary's-on-the-Quay.

St Mary's Catholic church ▣ on the far side of the busy centre is well worth a visit. At one time, only a hundred years ago, this church was also on the quayside, hence its name St Mary's on the Quay. It was designed by Richard Shackleton Pope as a chapel for the 'Catholic Apostolic Church' or 'Irvingites', a briefly fashionable evangelical sect, given to prophesy, glossolalia and predicting the end of the world in 1868. Like most grand Irvingite churches, incomplete, it was purchased by the Roman Catholics and opened in 1843 as they emerged from the obscurity of their Trenchard Street chapel in good time for the 'Papal Aggression' of 1850.

On leaving this church, turn left along the Centre and under the arcade to the cobbled area at the bottom of Christmas Steps. On the right corner, you will find the site of St Bartholomew's Hospital which you can enter through an arched stone passage.

The arch ▮ is also timber-framed. It led to the courtyard of the hospital, which was founded for elderly sailors in 1200. Note the mutilated statue of the Virgin within. (For further information see Walk 22.)

Climb Christmas Steps.

The steps were cut in 1669 to improve the steep route down to the bank of the River Frome. At the top left is the Chapel of the Three Kings, Melchior, Kaspar and Balthazar ▮▮. The traceried niches for their statues, modern replacements by Bristol sculptor Ernest Pascoe, can be seen over the door of Foster's Chapel. These almshouses are a Grade II listed building.

Cross Colston Street, turn right and cross Lower Park Row. Climb the steps in front of you, cross Perry Road and dead ahead you will find a stepped lane leading to Lower Church Lane. Directly ahead is St Michael's on the Mount Without.

'Without' implies that this church originally stood outside the City Wall - like the green hill faraway. The Georgian interior of this church ▣ was designed by Thomas Paty in 1775. It also has a very fine fifteenth century perpendicular tower. The Churchgoer found St Michael roomy but tame and poor. Its neighbourhood was no longer as aristocratic as it had been and 'Nebuchadnezzar might turn out to browse on the little streets that intersect the Old Park.'

In 1865, there was a strange commotion in the churchyard on the Feast of the Assumption of Our Lady. After Vespers, between one and two in the morning, the Third Order (local followers of Father Ignatius, the pseudo-Benedictine of Capel-y-fin in the Black Mountains) processed up the hill from their meeting room in Trenchard Street with lights and banners, singing a litany. This attracted an unruly crowd and the police had to break up the procession. (The police also had to intervene on another occasion when the Prior, Brother Cyprian, could not control two members of the order who tried to take part in a service when they were drunk. Refusing to do penance in white sheets, the drunkards were excommunicated amidst great uproar.)

Now walk down lower Church Lane, crossing St Michael's Hill at the traffic lights and into Upper Maudlin Street. Opposite the new Children's Hospital, beside Jameson's restaurant is Johnny Ball Lane.

The alley does not commemorate Wat Tyler's associate. It may be named after John à Ball, a mediaeval property owner who built the Bristol Bridge, which, like old London Bridge, was lined with shops. Then again, more plausibly, it may be an eighteenth century Johnny Ball.

The path goes round the old Infirmary paupers' graveyard. This was not a credit to the institution or the city. On one occasion the under-paid deputy chaplain kept a body waiting so long to be buried that the grave-diggers sent for him. He answered that he was otherwise engaged and could not come. Asked what to do with the body, he replied 'Put it in the tool house, I'll come tomorrow.' One of the undertakers read the service himself.

There were complaints that coffins were barely covered. The official response was that by digging graves 9'6" rather than 9' deep, six bodies could be placed in, making room for another 1,924 corpses in a space not much bigger than a cricket pitch.

Attempts by grave robbers to take anatomical specimens from the burial ground or the 'dead house', a coal hole lighted by a foot square iron grating, were not uncommon. Nurses were bribed to leave coffins open. Bodies were removed and replaced with earth or sand. A failed attempt led to a fist fight between medical students who had organised it. On another occasion soldiers in a hospital overlooking Johnny Ball Lane nearly shot two doctors. Then there was the episode of the purloined Negro's head that was dropped in the High Street and temporarily lost.

This long alley will take you back down to the city centre. Turn left and find the Unitarian church in Lewins Mead, marked 'Meeting Room'. Continue on to the bottom of Lower Maudlin Street. Turn left, cross the road and turn right to enter St James' Parade. Here you will find tucked away on the left St James' Church, also recommended for a visit.

St James' **L** was the parish church attended by the Wesleys. At the other Anglican extremity, Dr Pusey preached here once, though the bishop tried to dissuade the vicar from allowing him. (Pusey had Bristol connections: his daughters were educated in Clifton. Before Newman 'went over' to Rome, Pusey was welcome as a preacher at St Andrew's.)

When the famously rowdy St James' Fair was suppressed the church lost income. 'The application,' wrote a contemporary journalist, 'of the revenue arising from the Fair to the support of the Church was in my opinion the very next thing to the sale of Indulgences.'

*Turn right and follow a small lane cutting through St James' Park. Cross into Broadmead shopping centre via the pelican crossings and into Union Street. Turn left by Tesco Metro into Broadmead. Next to the Arcade, on the left, you will find John Wesley astride his horse outside the New Room **M**, the first Methodist chapel in the world, opened in 1739. At the Horsefair entrance is a statue of Charles Wesley. At the centre of Broadmead, turn right to pass the entrance to the Galleries shopping centre. At the end, turn right into Newgate (public conveniences on left) and climb to the top corner entrance to the Galleries opposite Castle Green. You will be using part of the Bristol Triangle, a Long Distance City Footpath. Look out for the distinctive yellow and green triangular* *waymarks as it leads you back, following the riverside, to Valentines Bridge and Temple Meads station. On Castle Green are the two blitzed churches, St Mary le Port and St Peter's (fourteenth century).*

Prominent now, in the nineteenth century St Mary le Port **N** was difficult to find 'packed up and thrust away somewhere to the rear of High Street.' The congregation was disturbed by the singing from the Bridge Street independent chapel. Congregational singing was said to be a great factor in the popularity of dissenting sects, providing 'an exciting influence on the rugged and undisciplined notions' of the lower orders.

St Peter's, another Norman and Perpendicular medley is perhaps on the site of Bristol's first religious foundation. The body of King Edmund rested here on its way to burial at Glastonbury Abbey. He was killed whilst trying to protect his steward from an attack by an outlaw at Pucklechurch.

Note the memorial to Savage who died whilst imprisoned for debt in Newgate Gaol, on the site of the Galleries. Savage had been well received in Bristol and given financial support, even when he exhausted local patience 'he suffered fewer hardships in prison than he had been accustomed to undergo in the greatest part of his life', being well treated by the standards of the day, indeed, by the standards of our own times: private room, frequent visits and walks in the fields. Mr Dagg the gaoler, praised as a pattern of benevolence by Savage's old friend Dr Johnson, kept him at his own expense. Savage's response was a satire on Bristol concluding with a charge against its citizens that Chatterton was to repeat.

Still spare the catamite and swinge the whore

And be whate'er Gomorrah was before.

Walk beside St Peter's Church and through the scented garden at the rear to follow the waterside path and up the steps to St Philip's Bridge. Go left to find at the corner of Tower Hill, the church of Ss Philip and Jacob.

Ss Philip and Jacob **O**, commonly named Pip and Jay. Here, the Churchgoer spent the service unsuccessfully trying to divert an illiterate young mother's whining baby by letting it play with his watch. In church, he was tempted to prefer a surly Siberian Bear to children.

Now cross Temple Way by the underpass, and turn right to walk along Temple Way. Turn left into Avon Street, opposite our starting point, Valentines Bridge, turn left into New Kingsley Road. On the left hand wall, at the corner with Old Bread Street, note a plaque to John Wesley. Continue on, then turn right into Jubilee Street through an alley to Barton Road. Turn right to find the Jewish cemetery opposite the Barley Mow pub. Perhaps there's just time for a couple of drinks before heading back.

The cemetery 🅿 was established early in the eighteenth century and leased until 1859 when the site was purchased. In 1990 it was renovated and it is still maintained by the burial society of the Bristol Hebrew Congregation. It was in Bristol that King John, a benefactor of the City, extorted tax from a Jew by extracting teeth.

Continue along Barton Road, turn right and right again into Avon Street. Opposite Kingsley Road, turn left to cross Valentines Bridge. The ferry stop is to your left, or return to Temple Meads station for the bus or train home.

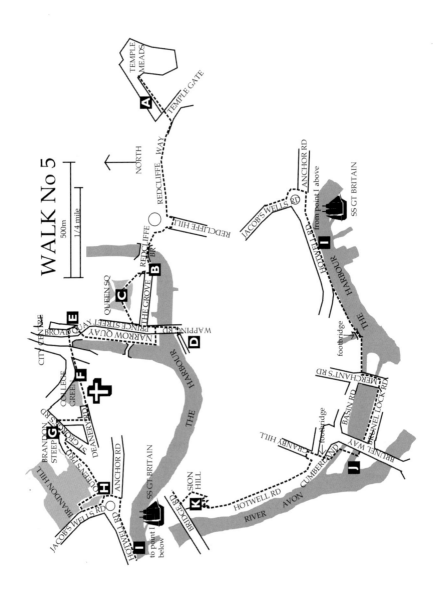

WALK No 5

500m
1/4 mile

NORTH

TEMPLE MEADS

TEMPLE GATE

A

REDCLIFFE WAY

REDCLIFFE HILL

JACOB'S WELLS

ANCHOR RD

SS GT BRITAIN

from point I above

HOTWELL RD

THE HARBOUR

CUMBERLAND RD

I

REDCLIFFE BR

B

QUEEN SQ

C

THE GROVE

WAPPING RD

NARROW QUAY

PRINCE STREET RD

D

BROAD QUAY

CITY CENTRE

E

COLLEGE GREEN

F

DEANERY RD

ST GEORGE'S RD

BRANDON STEEP

G

QUEEN'S RD

BRANDON HILL

JACOB'S WELLS RD

HOTWELL RD

H

ANCHOR RD

SS GT BRITAIN

I

to point I below

BRIDGE RD

SION HILL

K

HOTWELL RD

RIVER AVON

CUMBERLAND RD

BRANDY HILL

footbridge

BRUNEL WAY

BASIN RD

CHANNEL LOCK RD

MERCHANT'S RD

footbridge

THE HARBOUR

J

footbridge

BRUNEL'S FOOTSTEPS

Description: *This City Centre walk explores some of Isambard Kingdom Brunel's engineering projects in Bristol from 1829 to 1850, following a route from Temple Meads to the Clifton Suspension Bridge.*
Length: *3½ miles (2½-3 hours).*
Refreshments: *Numerous cafés and pubs along the route.*
Transport: *Bus nos 8 and 9 link Temple Meads and Clifton.*

Isambard (father's second name) Kingdom (his mother Sofia's maiden name) was born in Portsea, near Portsmouth on April 9th 1806. His first reported visit to the city was in 1828 for a long convalescence at the new Clifton and Hotwells Spas. This was following an accident in the tunnel his father, also an engineer, was building under the River Thames in London. On hearing the following year of the competition for a new Clifton Bridge, he returned to the city with four designs which were submitted by the 19th November. Thus began his 30 year commitment to Bristol. (His reputation did not always stand so high in the city as it does with posterity. John Latimer seldom has a good word for him, and describes him as 'an inexperienced theorist, enamoured of novelty, prone to seek for difficulties rather than to evade them, and utterly indifferent as to the outlay which his recklessness entailed upon his employers'.)

Begin at Temple Meads station **A** *walking down the Station Approach.*

The Old Station opened in 1840, designed by Brunel for wide gauge railways, and is the earliest surviving major rail terminus in the world. It is now the home of the Empire and Commonwealth Museum. A Grade I listed building in Tudor revival style housed the GWR offices and the train shed, at first floor level, which had the widest single span of the age, some 72 feet, with a mock timber hammerbeam roof. The left hand portal was the main entrance for pedestrians and carriages. An identical portal was demolished on the right hand side and was originally the main exit. It was last used by trains in 1965.

Cross Temple Gate, using pedestrian crossing, to view on the opposite side of the road the front of the Old Station. Turn left into Redcliffe Way and continue past St Mary Redcliffe Church, cross Redcliffe Hill and Redcliffe Bridge, turn left into The Grove **B**.

The Severn Shed, now a restaurant, is reputed to have a wrought iron structure designed by Brunel originally to test out his engineering design for Old Station.

Cross The Grove and into Queen Square **C**.

During the Bristol Riots in October 1831 Brunel was enlisted as a special constable and helped to salvage silver plate and pictures from the Mansion House, which was looted and destroyed by fire. He also gave evidence for the defence at the trial for negligence of Mayor Charles Pinney.

Turn left into Prince Street and cross bridge to Wapping Road **D**.

On the eastern gable of the Industrial Museum is a plaque commemorating the launch of the S.S. Great Western at Princes Wharf on the 19th July 1837. The timber-hulled paddle steamer designed by Brunel sailed to New York in April the following year. This was Brunel's dream of extending the railway with a steam ship to take passengers from London via Bristol to New York.

Retrace your steps back across bridge turn left and follow Narrow Quay to alongside harbour to Broad Quay **E**.

Brunel's Sculpture by John Doubleday was erected in 1982 at the same time as the seated version by the same sculptor at Paddington Station. In 1841 Brunel had completed the Great Western Railway from London to Bristol.

Walk across the City Centre to College Green **F**.

Brunel was invited by the Dean in 1850 to report on defects in the fabric of Bristol Cathedral. Brunel replied in his letter, 'I can be at the Cathedral at 5am on Tuesday morning next, having to leave Bristol by train to Exeter at 7·30am'. This gives an insight into Brunel's method and working hours!

Right to Park Street, then first left St George's Road **G**.

Brunel House, on the right hand side, built in 1837-39 to the designs of R.S. Pope and Brunel, was originally The Royal Western Hotel to provide overnight accommodation for rail travellers en route from London to New York. See plaque on south gable.

Turn right up Brandon Steep and along Queens Parade, noting harbour viewpoint at **H**. *Continue on footway to Brandon Hill and take steps on left to Jacob's Wells Road. Turn left to cross roundabout to south side of Hotwell Road* **I**.

From the dockside you can view Brunel's masterpiece, the SS *Great Britain*, launched by Prince Albert on 19th July 1843 becoming the world's first iron screw-driven steamship in the dry dock where she was constructed. The SS *Great Britain* left the harbour 18 months later as Brunel had to enlarge the Cumberland Basin Lock to take the vessel!

Follow harbour-side walk to Merchant's Road, turn left over bridge, then right along dockside parallel with Brunel Lock Road under Bridge, left to **J**.

The South Entrance Lock was completed by Brunel in 1849 with unique features: wrought-iron caisson single-leaf gates which were hollow and slightly buoyant at high water to make the heavy gate easier to operate, and an elliptical arch-shaped dock for self cleaning. Between the two locks, standing on the harbour, is the world's first wrought-iron tubular swing bridge. Designed by Brunel, he used similar construction later for the bridges at Chepstow and Saltash (Royal Albert Bridge).

Cross over North Lock Gates and through gate below Swing Bridge Control Tower, turn left along Cumberland Basin Road. Take footbridge over road, left Granby Hill, right Hotwell Road. After last houses and the old rock railway entrance turn right up zig-zag path to Sion Hill **K***.*

This is the viewpoint of Brunel's famous Clifton Suspension Bridge completed in 1864, spanning 630 feet of the Avon Gorge, based on the original competition design submitted in 1830. After funding problems the

bridge was completed in memory of Brunel who had died in 1859. Visit the Bridge and Visitor Centre for more information.

Walk along Bridge Road to Clifton Down Road for return bus 8 or 9 to City Centre and Temple Meads.

Footnote: interestingly there is no record of Brunel staying in the city over his 30 years of projects. It is thought that he either stayed in the GWR Office at Temple Meads or in a special rail carriage converted for his personal use. He lived over his office at 18 Duke Street, Westminster, and had a country house at St Marychurch, Devon.

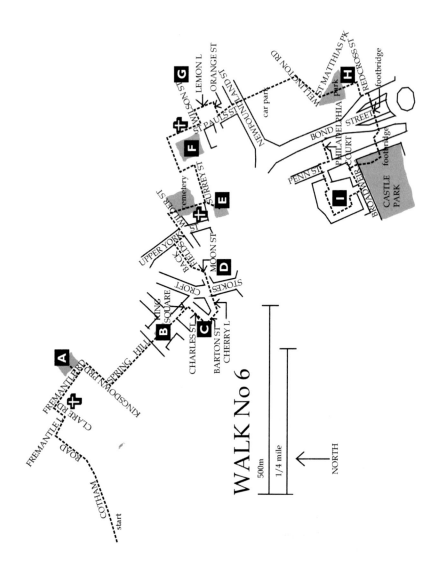

WALK No 6

500m

1/4 mile

NORTH

BRISTOL SQUARES

Description: *This walk goes through most of the squares of Kingsdown and St Paul's, finishing at Quakers Friars. It concentrates as much on former occupants - with an emphasis on medical history - as architecture. Many squares have been mutilated, though some damage was restored.*

Length: *3½ miles.*

Refreshments: *Cotham Porter Stores near the beginning (despite the name, a cider pub). Full Moon on Stokes Croft. The walk ends at Broadmead which has all the usual catering outlets.*

Transport: *8/9 buses link the start and finish. Many buses serve Broadmead.*

From the 8/9 bus stop on Cotham Road, go down the hill and turn right into Fremantle Lane, then left Clare Road, and right Fremantle Road into Fremantle Square.

The public objection to part of Fremantle's development is treated on Walk no 8. Now is the time to forget the old controversy, admire the square **A** itself and appreciate the renovation work of recent decades.

To leave Fremantle Square turn right along Apsley Villas and Kingsdown Parade. Turn left down Spring Hill. At the bottom is King Square.

King Square **B**, first known as New Square, was laid out in 1740 and named in honour of George II. Like most of the squares on the walk, it has not survived intact.

On the right hand side of the square, at No 3, a plaque commemorates Bristol's first medical school. In 1826, Mr Henry Clark set up the Bristol Medical and Surgical School. Two years later, his lectures were recognised by the Society of Apothecaries. For this reason, the badge of the Schola Medicinae in Bristol carries the date 1828. (Reversing the process whereby the American drug store began as a chemists and became a soda fountain, an apothecary's was first a sweet shop, then a pharmacy. By the early nineteenth century, an apothecary was roughly the equivalent of a modern GP; so, in 1815 the Society was given regulatory powers.) In 1833 several lecturers and staff from the Infirmary and the new General Hospital combined to found the Bristol Medical School which was housed in King Square till 1834 when it moved to Old Park.

To qualify, students had to spend six months in a London hospital. The Bristol Medical School resisted this on the grounds that 'Vast numbers of promising young men have had their characters, their usefulness and their peace of mind irreparably ruined by even a brief sojourn in the capital where practices of immorality and licentiousness may be persuaded with such great facility and so little immediate disgrace'. For the next mile you may reflect on the lost innocence of Stokes Croft and St Paul's.

John Wesley used to preach on the site of King Square. The indirect route from King Square to Stokes Croft takes you past the house where his younger brother lived between 1766-71 **C**. Charles was also a clergyman and a Methodist preacher, but he is best remembered as a hymn writer. The Wesleys were a musical family. Garret Wesley, Lord Mornington, who performed with Charles's children after they left Bristol, is reputed to have been the first member of the British aristocracy who dared to walk through the London streets openly and unashamedly carrying a violin case. He was a composer and Professor of Music at Trinity, Dublin, whilst his son Arthur's only indication of talent in youth was that he played well upon the fiddle. The Duke of Wellington (the variant Wellesley spelling is inexplicable) eventually displayed other abilities, but later in life he was a director of the pro-Handelian Concert of Ancient Music and indeed chose its last programme in 1848. Charles's sons, Charles and Samuel, 'the Mozart of Bristol', became prominent organists as did Samuel's illegitimate son Samuel Sebastian. Samuel was a worry to his family; at 21, he fell down a hole in the road and became a prey to mental aberrations. Even before this, he experimented with Catholicism.

Leaving the square by King Square Avenue turn right into Charles Street as far as Wesley's house. Turn back down Barton and Cherry Lane to Stokes Croft. Over the pedestrian crossing, go immediately left into Moon Street **D** *and right along Backfields, right Upper York Street, left Wilder Street and right through the Cemetery. Both the exits opposite lead to Brunswick Square.*

The Full Moon may be Bristol's second oldest pub site. It was the base for carriers serving south Gloucestershire. Here, the eighteenth century electorate was bribed with free dinners. (The candidate, standing against the American Cruger, perhaps the only man to be both an M.P. and a State Senator, invited the enfranchised to try the difference between the roast beef of Old England and American bull beef.) In the fields behind, the West Gloucestershire Cricket Club played its first match in 1854. All England won by 149 runs: probably because, at 6, W.G. Grace was too young to play. He was watching and remembered some of the All England players wearing tall hats. The Coroner's Court building is a former school.

Brunswick Square **E** was never completed. Arguably, the Unitarian burial ground was discouraging. The headstone of John Latimer, the journalist and annalist, is said to be here. There is also a monument to him in the Cathedral. The Grecian chapel was built for the Unitarians. Unitarianism became well established amongst well educated dissenters. Early in the nineteenth century it seemed set to become the chief rival to the established church. At one point in the eighteenth century most members of the Corporation were claimed to be Unitarian.

The place names of central Bristol are an intriguing study. The street naming classes obviously tried hard to keep up with political change and to gratify local vanity. So there are Marlborough and Prince Eugene, from the days of Good Queen Ann; Brunswick, to mark the Hanoverians. If Orange Street is political, Lemon Lane must be a joke. Cave Street commemorates a Bristol banking family, not a hole in the ground. Deceptively, Portland was not King Billy's boyfriend, but a later eighteenth century duke, High Steward of the City. His sumptuous portrait by Thomas Lawrence is in the City Art Gallery. Wade is also a trap: not the general who built roads in Scotland, but Nathaniel, the town clerk who developed the site. Peaching on his fellow rebels after Monmouth's Uprising made him unpopular, hence the name of 'Traitor's Bridge'.

Leave by Surrey Street, left Portland Square **F**.

The Churchgoer found St Paul's church dusty and plagued by a riotous set of boys whom the schoolmaster tried to control by prodding them throughout the service with his umbrella. What he really needed for the task was a Russian knout. The sermon was colloquial to the point of being undignified. As for the architecture, it was 'peculiar', the spire inspired by an oriental tea tray.

Built in 1794 and fashionable for a while, socially, the square had gone down by the mid-nineteenth century. It was said to be insalubrious. This is very, very plausible as the site is low lying, to the east of the city, near the Frome but another theory retailed to Joseph Leech was that the inhabitants might have lived to the age of Methuselah; what drove people away was the gossip. 'Squares are ever most subject to the influence of scandal.'

Leave by Wilson Street in the top right hand corner.

Wilson Street **G**, named after an eighteenth century Bishop who is otherwise forgotten, was for a time the home of the Blackwell family. Samuel Blackwell was a remarkable man, partly for his advanced views on female equality, partly, despite his trade of sugar refiner, for his opposition to slavery. After emigrating to America, he experimented with sugar beet as an alternative to the cane produced by slave labour. His house, No 1 Wilson Street, was later acquired by George Müller, who had opened his first orphanage at No 6 and aimed to run his charities by the efficacy of prayer without appealing for money. Rivals in this field of charity said he cheated.

In her autobiography, Blackwell's daughter Elizabeth recalled her Bristol childhood: 'The group of brothers and sisters grew up together, taking daily walks with our governess into the lovely environs of the then small town. We became familiar with the St Vincent's Rocks and the Hot Wells, with Clifton Down and Leigh Woods, which were not built on then. The Suspension Bridge across the Avon was a thing of the future, and Cook's Folly stood far away on the wild Durdham Down.

'All these neighbourhoods were delightfully free and open. Our governess encouraged our natural tastes, and the children's pennies were often expended in purchasing the landscape stones and Bristol diamonds offered for sale on Clifton Down. In still another direction, the "Brook" leading through pleasant fields to the distant Beaufort woods had a never ending charm.'

Elizabeth grew up to fame as the first woman on the British Medical Register having studied and qualified in America. She returned to Bristol in 1869 for the annual meeting of the National Association for the

Promotion of Social Science. On the agenda was a debate on the Contagious Diseases Acts, an attempt to control pox in the armed forces by the compulsory examination of suspected prostitutes in garrison towns and naval bases. From this women were excluded, but Elizabeth Blackwell, as a doctor, could attend, so she was briefed by Mary Carpenter, the educationalist reformer, to put the case against. She was relieved when Cardinal Newman's brother took the lead in the debate, which ended in a resolution calling for the repeal of the Acts.

Turn right down Lemon Lane right along Orange Street, left and left into St Paul Street to Newfoundland Street. Over the crossing, go straight ahead to Wellington Road. Cut through the park and turn right, Redcross Street ▣.

A plaque marks the birthplace of Thomas Lawrence, the fashionable portrait painter and president of the Royal Academy. Soon after Thomas's birth in 1769, his father, who had kept the famous White Lion in Broad Street, moved to Devizes to run the Bear Inn. A child prodigy, at the age of twelve, Thomas Lawrence had a studio in Bath. In his early twenties, he was appointed Limner to George III.

Timothy Mowl, the astringent commentator on Georgian Bristol, remarks that the two blocks of maroon coloured concrete on either side of this dramatic relic of a baroque terrace are like brutalist ear muffs on a delicate face. The reflective glass of the top storey adds sinister shades.

Turn right into Bond Street and cross by the footbridge. Go through the multi-storey car park and cross the next footbridge into Castle Park. Follow the edge of the park to the right and, over the pedestrian crossing at Broad Weir, turn left and right into Quakers Friars ▮.

To your right as you crossed the dual carriage way was the site of the lost square, St James', destroyed to make way for a new road Bond Street, which some analysts regard as the root cause of central Bristol's planning and social problems.

Castle Park is a useful open space in the city's centre, but by no means a formally planned square. The bombed-out churches and the statues are described in Walks no 3 and 4. Interpretative panels on the site explain the remains of Bristol Castle.

The bad old days of planning that carved up the city centre with the inhuman ring road also account for the wretched state of Quakers Friars. If all goes well, the dustbins and car parks that surround the mediaeval building will disappear with the development of a new square.

The Friars, Dominicans, came in the thirteenth century. As a relic, they acquired a footprint of Jesus Christ, on marble. The remains of their building was the hall; the church did not survive. In 1540 the vibrations of gunfire at the castle brought down the tower. The Quakers bought the site in 1747 for their first meeting house in Bristol.

Note the street names commemorating William Penn, the Quaker founder of Philadelphia and his wife's family Callowhill. Philadelphia Street itself, locally rendered Phillyify Street, like other roads lost in redevelopment gave its name to a court.

Go clockwise round the central building and leave by the alley at '3 o'clock'. Cross Penn Street and turn right and left down Philadelphia Court, then left to bus stop.

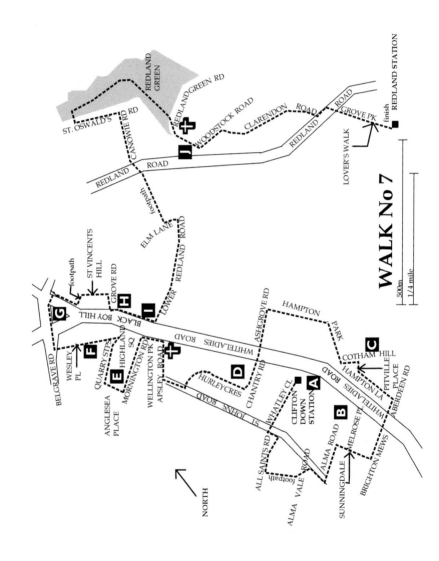

WALK No 7

CLIFTON - REDLAND

Description: Clifton and Redland are usually thought of as pleasant and respectable eighteenth and nineteenth century suburbs. This walk concentrates on their commercial and industrial aspects: railways, quarries, lime kilns, nursery gardens and old road patterns.

Length: 3½ miles.

Refreshments: Many pubs and cafés on the first part of the walk. Nothing en route beyond Blackboy Hill.

Transport: Trains on the Severn Beach railway and the No 8/9 bus link the start and finish. Many buses serve Whiteladies Gate.

The Walk starts from Clifton Down railway station.

Clifton Down **A**, opened 1874, though now ruined by development and neglect, was once a handsome station served by trains to Temple Meads and, over the Midland line, to Mangotsfield and Bath. The likelihood of a station on Whiteladies Road was an important factor when Bristol Grammar School moved to its present site. The school hoped to extend its catchment area along the line towards Bath. Originally, Clifton Down Tunnel was to be built to Brunel's broad gauge (the section was run jointly by the Midland and Great Western companies) but this was found to be too expensive. Spoil from the tunnel may well have been used to build the red stone retaining wall opposite the station's main entrance. The University's Canynge building on the other side of the approach road used to be the Imperial Hotel, serving the station.

Past the old station buildings (now a pub) turn left along St John's Road, right into All Saints Road, and take the footpath on the left to Alma Vale Road. Turn left back to St John's Road, then right to Alma Road, left and take third turning right along Sunningdale.

To your left down Melrose Place **B**, note the façade of Whiteladies Picture House, the first purpose built cinema in Bristol, where young ladies literally swooned at Rudolf Valentino. The architect, La Trobe, seems to have had a fancy for decorative façades on the sides of buildings. He was

responsible also for an ornate blind wall you will see later in Lower
Redland Road. Recently, big business closed the cinema.

*At the end of Melrose Avenue, go left along Brighton Mews, cross Whiteladies
Road, turn into Aberdeen Road and follow Hampton Lane on the left as far as
the obscure entry into Pitville Place on the right.*

From its name, Pitville Place dates from the early nineteenth century but
the terrace is said to be 1850. Like the 1840 Hampton Terrace in Hampton
Park it must have had a conservative architect. Many cities have their own
terms for an alleyway like this that only pedestrians can use: snickets,
shuts, ginnels, jiggers. (In Liverpool, a jigger rabbit is or was a cat.) Not in
colloquial use, 'back' is probably the nearest Bristolian equivalent.

*Pitville Place leads to Cotham Hill, turn left and right up Hampton Park, at the
top go left, Ashgrove Road, cross Whiteladies Road to Chantry Road.*

Cotham Hill **C** was the main road from Bristol to the Aust Ferry. The
route was a toll road, gated at the junction with Whiteladies Road, which the
Turnpike Trustees constructed to avoid St Michael's Hill. To prevent evasion,
Whiteladies Road and Redland Lane (now Hampton Road) were also gated.

At No 3 Hampton Park lived Samuel Loxton whose drawings are the
classic record of Edwardian Bristol.

Hatches in the small car park opposite the phoney Irish pub give access
to the Northern Stormwater Interceptor, a seven and a half mile long,
tunnel 16 feet in diameter, running 285 feet deep to discharge into the
Avon near Black Rock Quarry.

Before this area was developed in the mid-nineteenth century, there were
orchards, limepits and nursery gardens. The last fragment of the nurseries is
Garraways **D**, larger in the 1840s, when Chilcott's guide-book says that
independent of the pleasure to be derived from the plant collection, it was 'through
the liberality of the proprietors quite a promenade for respectable visitors'.

*Right and round Hurle Crescent, right along St John's Road, right, Apsley Road
to Blackboy Hill. (Lovers of pink churches may pause in delight at the former
St John's, now an auction room.) Go up the hill as far as Wellington Park, from
which right into Mornington Road, and right at the end up Anglesea Place.*

A plaque commemorates the brief residence in Anglesea Place **E** of the music hall star, Randolph Sutton, famous for the doleful 'On Mother Kelly's Doorstep' which he said he got from his milkman. Sutton broke with the tradition of British Pantomime to become the first male Principal Boy.

Worrall Road was named for one of the local family who suffered the indignant, but futile reprobation of the Council for developing the site, popularly considered to form part of Clifton Down. Other street names, Apsley, Wellington, Mornington, Hughenden, Beaconsfield suggest Tory sympathies. Despite the developers' politics, this district was missionary territory; the Church of England and the Congregationalists competing to save the 'spiritually destitute' quarrymen, thieves and prostitutes by building two schools, a church (St John's) and a Mission Hall. The school at the corner of Anglesea Place was set up by the Highbury Congregationalists, though it later became an annex to St John's C. of E. Primary. A fragment of the Victorian building was preserved by a strange planning compromise when the new school was imposed on the townscape.

Cross to Sutherland Place, right up Quarry Steps. (To avoid the steps go left and right up Richmond Dale.) Go right along High Street to Highland Square.

The prospect from the top of Quarry Steps **F**, shows how unchecked quarrying and development might have left the whole of the Downs. In 1724, there was concern that quarrying had made the paths dangerous. A mid-nineteenth century guidebook warned walkers on near the Gorge not 'to approach too near the margin of the rocks, as an explosion of the gunpowder used in blasting the rocks may possibly throw some stones on your path'. The familiar level appearance of the Downs is due to environmental improvements in the 1870s. When Cumberland Basin was remodelled and Round Point and Tea and Coffee House Point were removed in an attempt to make navigation easier, the spoil was taken along a tramway by the river, hauled up an inclined plane by a stationery engine and used to fill in three big quarries. The bottom of the inclined plane disappeared in later quarry work in the Gorge, but the top can still be traced, parallel with Circular Road. The engine must have stood near the Gully.

The striking coloured-brick building is Amberley Hall, built by the Congregationalists to spread temperance, music. and family life.

Leave Highland Square by Wesley Place to the right of the Coach and Horses.

Householders near the Downs used to let out front rooms to football clubs before the changing rooms were built.

The grassy islands **G** at the top of the slope were the terminus of tram lines from the Centre and Eastville.

The former St John's School, now a nest of social workers, was one of the last encroachments on the common land of the Downs.

Cross Blackboy Hill, noting the hospital in another old quarry. Go right down the hill, noting the fancy urinal and the fountain commemorating Uriah Rees Thomas, a local Congregationalist minister and man of Good Works. Left up the steps before the filling station.

The Cottages on St Vincent's Hill **H** are another relic of the area's industrial, mining, quarrying and lime-burning past. The scattered layout is characteristic of the early industrial revolution.

Follow the path to Grove Road, right to the Blackboy and down the hill. (Woodbury Lane is a tempting dead end.) Left into Lower Redland Road.

Like Whiteladies Road, Blackboy Hill was named after a pub, but not the one on this corner, which was till recently the 'Elephant and Castle' ∎. The real 'Blackboy Inn', earlier the 'Blackamoor's Head', was sited further up until it was removed on the familiar grounds of traffic flow in 1878. (There is no connection with the slave trade. Like the barracoons in the Redcliffe Caves, this is a romantic invention.) Opposite is the La Trobe façade mentioned above. He also designed the terracotta buildings at the top of Blackboy Hill.

The direct route is straight along Lower Redland Road, but it is worth diverting round Redland Terrace and West Shrubbery.

Once again, the scale of the quarry workings is obvious. The Police Station used to house the mounted section of the force. The buildings at the back were police houses.

The meaning of 'Redland' is disputed. Possibly the obvious explanation from the soil colour is correct, but 'red', like the Yorkshire 'riding' may derive from 'thrid', a tri-partite division. An eighteenth century road atlas spells the name as 'Ridland; and 'thrid' is fairly certainly the derivation of 'Durdham'. Then again, the name may mean 'cleared land'.

From the bottom of Elm Lane, take the footpath on the right up to Redland Road, cross, turn into Canowie Road, take the second left St Oswald's Road, and follow the path on the right to Redland Green. Cross the Green and take the path to the right past the playground to the Church.

On Elm Lane lived William Metford who served as an engineer on the Bristol and Exeter Railway, became involved in the Indian Mutiny, invented, with J.P. Lee, the standard army rifle and, on his own, an explosive rifle bullet which was internationally banned.

The green lasted long in agricultural use. Cattle grazed before the Bishop's Palace (bombed in the War), and the farmhouse sold teas to Sunday walkers. The remarkable English Baroque Redland Church ∎ was built as a private chapel for Redland Court.

Beyond the church, follow Woodstock Road to the left and turn left down Clarendon Road to the 8/9 bus stops or continue along Lovers Walk (Grove Park) to the railway station (see Walk no 8). This is part of the Bristol Triangle urban long distance walk.

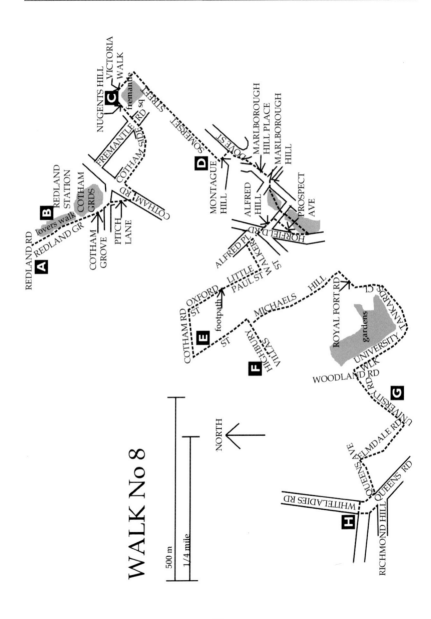

WALK No 8

REDLAND - CLIFTON

Description: *Resistance to development did not begin in 1963. This walk visits sites that were controversial in the eighteenth and nineteenth centuries.*
Length: *3 miles.*
Refreshments: *Pubs and cafés on St Michael's Hill. Cotham Porter Stores.*
Transport: *Many buses run to Queens Road. Nos 8, 9 serve the start of the walk. No 9 links the beginning and end. Redland station is near the beginning and Clifton Down half a mile from the end.*

Begin at the junction of Redland Road and Redland Grove **A**.

Elizabeth Blackwell, the first woman doctor in America whose childhood passed in Bristol in the 1820s, recalled in her autobiography 'Mother Pugsley's field, with its healing spring, leading out of Kingsdown Parade, was a favourite walk - for passing down the fine avenue of elms we stood at the great iron gates of Sir Richard Vaughan's place to admire the peacocks, and then passed up the lane towards Redland, where violets grew on the grassy banks and natural curiosities could be collected.' Sir Richard Vaughan's place is now Redland High School. It still has the gates. If you are a Betjemanesque voyeur, you may prefer young ladies at tennis to peacocks, otherwise, you may regard the courts as a barbarous intrusion on a Palladian setting.

In 1829 Sir Richard, a banker, was dispossessed of his pavonian splendour by a bank, having got into financial difficulties over property speculation at Tyndall's Park. A singularly unendearing M.P. named Bailie, a slave-owning Scotsman whose family believed the English poor should live on oatmeal dumplings, bought the property. At his death in 1863 he was selling the estate off as building lots. His executors sold Lovers Walk in two parcels. George Thomas (a Quaker philanthropist who also helped save Leigh Woods from speculative development) and others came to an agreement with the new owners so the trees in the Grove **B** were not felled. In 1879, two of the Fry family conveyed four acres of Lovers Walk to the Corporation; the adjoining land was enclosed as a pleasure ground.

Follow Lovers Walk in Grove Park past Redland Station and Cotham Gardens. Follow Cotham Grove, and Pitch Lane, the alley which is probably the old path, cross Cotham Road, turn left and a little way down the hill turn right into Cotham Side, leading to the junction of Fremantle Road and Nugents Hill.

Mother Pugsley was a civil war widow, fond of children, who died at the age of 80 and by her own request was 'borne forth on an open bier, dressed in her marriage garments and with her wedding sheet for a winding one, the bells of St Nicholas ringing merrily as the coffinless corpse passed under the gate, and a fiddler playing a lively tune in front.' She was buried in the field which bore her name; her husband had been shot and buried there. The field became a popular playground. The well was supposed to be good for the eyes. (Joseph Leech, a nineteenth century journalist, refers to the 'one eye' of the tradesman, wearied with always being open: a long-lasting Bristolian joke.)

In 1839, although pedestrians had enjoyed access from time immemorial to the spring in Pugsley's Field **C**, 'to use the language of a local journalist [Leech again] Sir Thomas Fremantle, the owner of the land, flourished his title deed in the face of the public and nobody had the spirit to defend the rights of the community.'

One development was prevented by the bankruptcy of the developer and there was talk of making the fields more attractive than ever, 'building over and beautifying the well' but in the end the site was not protected and in the early 1840s another scheme went ahead. No trace of the well remains. Revisiting her native city, Elizabeth Blackwell was disappointed to find it gone.

Turn right off Nugents Hill into Victoria Walk. Leave Fremantle Square by Somerset Street, and turn left down Montague Hill, the stepped lane just before you get to West End **D**.

The affair of Mother Pugsley's well was by no means the first dispute over the development of Kingsdown. In 1760 people were complaining about greedy developers enclosing the down and spoiling the view. An appeal for a public subscription to preserve the site failed. This environmental outrage was poetically described and assigned its place in the class struggle.

A Soliloquy on Kingsdown

O! WHAT a wretched Chaos art thou made
Once lovely KINGSDOWN! Nature's sweet Parade!
Deep Trenches now deform thy Walks once fair
And smoky Lime kilns taint thy healthy Air:
Huge Heaps of Stones, and Mortar scab thy Brow
For building Plebean [sic] Seats for nought but Show.
Come hither Pedlars, quit your dusty stalls.
Here build your Seats, on rise your garden walls.
And when you've built it e'er call it what you will
'Twill not be Kingsdown then, but Pedlars Hill.

The next section of the walk takes you through the remains of this development, and displays some of the atrocities that replaced it.

At the foot of Montague Hill turn right along Dove Street into Marlborough Hill Place, cross Marlborough Hill and take the footpath, cross Alfred Hill and go on up the eleven steps to Horfield Road. (Note the plaque of a centaur and a faun on the wall opposite.) Turn right and right again along Prospect Avenue, then left up Alfred Hill. Cross to Alfred Place, go left along Walker Street, right into Little Paul Street and straight through the High Kingsdown development, passing the play area on the way, to Oxford Street which leads to Cotham Road. Turn left to the top of St Michael's Hill 🇪.

This is the site of one of the City's places of public execution. The nimbies of 1773 complained that the crowds at this entertainment were damaging their property and asked that the gallows be erected on Brandon Hill instead. Note the plaque on the Church commemorating the Marian Martyrs who were burned, or rather suffocated with smoke with damp wood, nearby. The Church is now used by the Church of England, but it was designed for the Congregationalists by Butterfield, generally considered an Anglican architect. He is said to have regretted it for the rest of his life, but this was his first commission and his nonconformist uncle was paying for the project.

A minister's missionary son told the story of a Maori convert who disappeared. The explanation from the other converts was, 'he gave us so much good advice, we had to eat him.'

Turn left down St Michael's Hill and after the zebra crossing detour right into Highbury Villas **F**.

The modest terrace shields the original villas (formerly Albert Villas) behind. 'Highbury' derives from the London suburb. The chapel was called after the dissenting college there.

Having seen the unsympathetic building perpetrated by Bristol Corporation and the hospitals, on the next section of the walk you can appreciate the impact of the university.

Return to St Michael's Hill, turn right and right into Royal Fort Road, left along Tankards Close, passing the School of Medical Science, and University Walk. (A detour into the gardens of Royal Fort is highly recommended) **G**.

Both the Senate House to your right and the Geography Faculty in University Road were built on Botanic Gardens. A few specimen trees still remain. An inscription from Hippocrates, over the door of the Geography Faculty, **O ΒΙΟΣ ΒΡΑΧΥΣ Η ΔΕ ΤΕΧΝΗ ΜΑΚΡΗ**, 'the life so short, the craft so long to learn', dates from its time as the Medical School.

Woodland Road follows the line of an ancient footpath 'Cut Throats' Lane' diverted in 1860.

Tyndalls Park, stretching from Park Row to Cotham Hill and from Whiteladies Road to St Michael's Hill, was laid out in the mid-eighteenth century mostly on land leased from the Corporation and the Dean and Chapter. Development of the site began in 1792, but like many such projects in Bristol, the scheme foundered during the war-time slump in the housing market. In 1794 the elder Thomas Tyndall died and the younger Thomas Tyndall bought in the estate at auction. He planted trees to shut out the view of the couple of houses that had been built, and put some mounds around the public footpaths that ran through the estate.

In 1844 Thomas Onesiphorus Tyndall tried to develop part of the estate. This came to nothing, but by his death in 1869 most of the land had been sold off for building.

Take University Road to your left. Turn right along Elmdale and left on Queen's Avenue. The No 9 bus back to the start of the walk stops outside Habitat, but cross Queens Road to Richmond Hill first and look back, noticing the R.W.A., the Victoria Rooms and the Boer War memorial **H**.

In 1852 land was taken from Tyndall's Park to widen Whiteladies Road to the left. The elm trees in the park were left along the roadside. This became a favourite Sunday evening promenade for the 'youthful working classes of both sexes', so happily, when the elms were felled in 1865, they were replaced by plane trees.

The plot of land to the left has an instructive history. In 1856, the local residents determined to have some hovels and 'petty shops' removed and an ornamental garden laid out. The land was bought by public subscription and conveyed to the Merchant Venturers subject to certain conditions, with the intention that it be kept as open space for all time. In 1934, the Clerk to the Society looked into the restrictive covenants and reported that the Society was under no such legal obligation although he thought there might be a moral obligation. Faced with Press criticism, the Society decided not to let the land for building. In 1954 there was another scheme and in 1955 in collusion with the insatiable University of Bristol, the Society applied for planning permission. When the application was refused, it sought compensation and received £28,000.

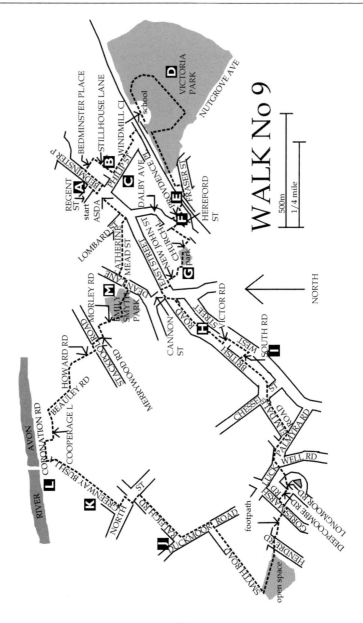

WALK No 9

HISTORIC BEDMINSTER

Description: *A mix of the old and the new; from lead, smoke and coal to green pastures and sustainable buildings. A 2 hour walk through some older, greener, and unusually interesting parts of South Bristol. Bedminster was once a major industrial town in Somerset and part of the Bristol coalfield. It is now a mixture of old housing, some new workplaces, and has some usually unexplored green spaces, back alleys and footpaths.*

Length: *4 miles circular.*

Refreshments: *Available from several public houses and daytime cafés (not Sundays); ASDA has a café; Windmill Hill City Farm has a daytime café.*

Transport: *Buses 88-9, 75, 76, 77 all stop at Bedminster Parade. Bedminster railway station is en route.*

Start from Bedminster Library at the junction of Regent Road and Bedminster Parade. (If arriving by train, an alternative start and finish is at Bedminster station.)

Bedminster Library **A** was opened in 1877 when the Corporation bought it for £1500 from the 'defunct' Conservative Institute.

Cross Bedminster Parade at the pedestrian crossing. Turn left, past Taunton Leisure shop (discount for Ramblers members!). Turn right at the second 'tunnel' into Bedminster Place, opposite the old stone police station. Turn right at the end into Stillhouse Lane.

In Bedminster Place and Stillhouse Lane **B** were some of the less desirable old houses in Bedminster. The slums were demolished about 40 years ago. These cobbled streets were home to hundreds who suffered cholera in the 1840s. In 1849, it was reported that Bedminster had a pile of 'continuous scrapings a quarter of a mile long and 5 feet high'. (Don't look too close now.)

Willway Street (to the left) has a former malthouse/distillery, currently (2001) used as a nightclub.

Turn left at the junction at the end into Philip Street.

Philanthropist John James was born in Philip Street. Across to the right is Windmill Hill City Farm **C**.

At the end turn left and cross the pedestrian crossing into Windmill Close; go under the railway bridge and bear left keeping the railway to your left and the school to the right. Enter Victoria Park; take the steep path to the right to the ridge. Rest if you wish to take in the city-wide panorama. Follow the path in a circle round to your right to the southwest side.

Victoria Park **D** was laid out in 1888; the land was bought from the Smyth family by the Corporation of Bristol for £50,000; there was a windmill on this farmland which gave the area its name.

Keep the houses to your left and follow the paths back to the top; then take the path downhill past the antique lamppost towards the railway. Turn left at the railway along the path behind the houses in Fraser Street. Turn right into Fraser Street.

Fraser Street and the houses nearby were built for the workers at the smelting works owned by Alfred Capper Pass.

Bedminster Railway station **E** is on the Bristol to Exeter line first opened in 1841 and later taken over by GWR. The first station on this site (the original Bedminster station lay 250 yards east) was opened in 1884. This decorative building was replaced when the track was quadrupled in 1933. The murals at the entrance off Fraser Street were painted in 2001; notice the recently made flower garden.

Turn right and proceed under the railway bridge. Cross the pedestrian crossing at Hereford Street/Whitehouse Lane. Bear left onto a footpath next to the cycle track alongside the wooden building.

This is the GreenHouse **F**, headquarters of the Federation of City Farms and Community Gardens.

A Mill existed here until Victorian times on the Malago river, which now flows under Providence Place (the green) since it was diverted after disastrous floods in 1882 and 1889. In 1882 Hereford Street was under 8 feet of water, and 1000 houses were flooded.

The Capper Pass lead works were built in Providence Place in the 1840s and closed in the 1960s. Next door was Cox's tannery and lots of houses (now demolished) on land which is now the City Farm. (Can you spot Little Paradise?)

Turn left at Dalby Avenue and cross at the pedestrian crossing. Turn left along Dalby Avenue and take the second right turn at Church Lane opposite Pring and St Hill factory.

Pring and St Hill steel works dates from 1921 but had earlier been part of Sampsons foundry (from 1872) associated with a nearby brickworks.

Cross to the other side of Church Lane and take the steps behind the red brick flats into the former St John's churchyard.

St John's Church **G** was originally built in Charles II's time in the seventeenth century. A new church was built here in 1855. It was bombed in World War II and demolished in the 1960s.

Cross to the right side of this small park and leave via the gate. Turn left onto the footpath and then right at the end into New John Street past the former Robinson's building. Follow this narrow road, keeping the redbrick Robinson building to the left into Norfolk Place; between the buildings and down steps into East Street. Turn left; cross over at the traffic lights.

Robinson's printers (1887) is now part of Cameron's Balloon factory. The Robert Fitzharding pub (to your right in Cannon Street) was named after the landowner of the Bedminster area. He was the Earl of Gloucester and Lord Berkeley. His family took over the land from the Crown in the eleventh century. Henry VIII later claimed it back, but the estate was granted to the Smyth family of Ashton Court in 1605. Their wealth was secured by the discovery of coal later in the eighteenth century. Most of the pits in the South Bristol area were on their land.

Cross over Cannon Street to the London Inn and into British Road.

British Road **H** was the site of the original local Methodist church and the associated British School (mostly destroyed by a recent fire). A breakaway church was built in Hebron Road (to the right), where twelve cholera victims are buried. Note also the handsome Albert Cottage (1846).

Continue for about half a mile and turn left at Victor Road. Turn right into West Street. Take the second right turn, into South Road opposite Argus Road. Turn left, back into British Road.

West Street has two former miners' pubs, the Jolly Colliers and the Red Cow, which was an alternative name for the Malago Pit otherwise known as the Argus Pit. The former pit manager's cottage is still there on the corner of Argus Road ∎ (subject to a recent modernisation!). Ten miners died in a gas explosion at this pit in 1891.

South Street School (on the right) dates from School Board days; a famous old boy is Chris Garland formerly of Bristol City F.C.

Turn right at the end into Chessel Street and immediately left into Elmdale Road Turn right at the next crossroads to the Luckwell pub on your left. Cross over Luckwell Road and take the footpath between houses on the opposite (west) side. Veer right into Longmoor Road then turn right into Deepcombe Road. Turn left at the end and cross to the left onto Gore's Marsh Road. Turn right at the first footpath between houses. Keep to the centre with new houses to the left and garden walls to the right. At the end of the footpath cross over Hendre Road onto the Gore's Marsh open space.

At Gore's Marsh was New Deep Pit, 294 yards deep. This mine was typical in that it flooded regularly, and eventually proved uneconomic. Disused pits were used in 1845 to pump up water for drinking; 160,000 gallons a day were brought up in this way. Other Ashton coal mines were at South Liberty Lane and Ashton Vale.

Turn right at the next road (Smyth Road). At the crossroads (about half a mile) turn left onto Duckmoor Road. Cross over to the other side and turn right at Raleigh Road. At the top of the gradual incline turn left onto North Street. Cross over at the pedestrian crossing opposite the Tobacco Factory.

The redbrick buildings were the main factory of W.D. & H.O. Wills, closed in the 1970s, now a theatre and new restaurant ∎.

Turn left and take the first right (Greenway Bush Lane) after the supermarket. Stay on Greenway Bush Lane for about two-thirds of a mile.

Walter Street (to the left) has a few recently self-built wooden frame houses based on the Walter Segal method **K**. In Greenway Bush Lane is the site of the Sydney Pit.

Turn right at the end onto Coronation Road opposite Ashton Gate post office.

Coronation Road **L** was opened by Lady Smyth in 1822 to mark the coronation of William IV; the ceremony was preceded by her husband Captain Smyth leading a coach and four with a team of his private yeoman soldiers; they were later to see real action during the Bristol Riots in 1831. One of the first events of the 1831 riots was a protest at the then new St Paul's church in Coronation Road, led by Christopher Davies of the Political Union; the crowd threw stones and fought police in anger at the Bishop's rejection of the Reform Bill. On 27th January 1832, William Clarke, son of the landlord of the Hen and Chicken pub in North Street, Bedminster (also a local timber yard owner), was hanged at Bristol Prison for his part in the arson of the Mansion House in Queen Square.

Turn right after about 200 yards into Cooperage Lane and bear left between garages and houses. At the end, turn right and cross over Beauley Road. After half a mile, turn left into Howard Road; bear right up the hill and turn left into Stackpool Road. Cross over into the first right (at Merrywood Road) and immediately left into Morley Road. At the far end, go through the metal gate entrance to Dame Emily play area and park. There are usually murals to admire here on the right hand wall! Cross the play area towards the central circular area, down the steps to the path leading to the entrance gate alongside the swimming baths.

Dame Emily Smyth Park is the site of Dean Lane colliery **M**. The pit shaft is under the circular area that was once the bandstand. Eight miners were killed and ten injured in an explosion here in 1886. The mine closed before the First World War following a wage demand by the union. The last Bedminster pit to close was South Liberty Lane in 1925.

Turn left onto Dean Lane; cross at the pedestrian crossing.

The pub opposite used to be known as the Clarence and was used by miners.

Shortly, turn right into Catherine Mead Street. At the redbrick HQ of Imperial Tobacco, turn right into Lombard Street and immediately left, back into Bedminster Parade. Keep to the left. Bedminster library is a further 100 yards.

Just a few facts about Bedminster:
- Bedminster rose dramatically in population from 4,577 in 1811 to 34,751 in 1885.
- Every Easter, until Victorian society stopped it, Bedminster was the scene of 'rude festivity ... and low debauchery, known by the name of the 'Bedminster Revels'.
- In November 1822 police arrested five people for 'body-snatching' in a Bedminster churchyard.
- In August 1820, a man and two boys were flogged through the streets of Bedminster for stealing fruit from a garden.
- In 1849 there was not one street light in Bedminster or St Philip's.
- Mr W.D. Wills survived the effects of his cigarettes (if he smoked them) but was unequal to the weight of a London bus; he was knocked down by one and lost his life in 1865.

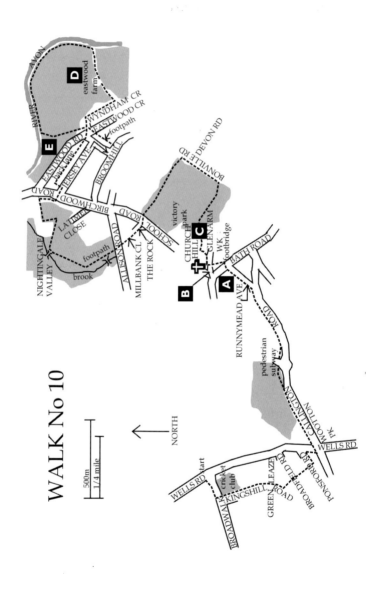

BEESE'S TEA GARDEN

Description: A mainly flat suburban walk, taking you through Brislington Village, Victory Park, St Anne's Woods and Eastwood Nature Reserve. At certain times of the year, it is possible to cross the Avon by ferry from Beese's Tea Garden to Conham River Park opposite for around 25p.

Length: 4 miles linear.

Refreshments: Tesco's superstore, White Hart pub, Brislington Hill. Good Intent, Broomhill Road. Beese's Tea Garden open March-September.

Transport: Bus no 1 runs from Broomhill Road to the Centre. Buses 36, 51, 52, 54, 55 serve Broad Walk shops. Bus no 36 links Broad Walk with St Anne's Park Road.

From outside the shopping centre entrance at the junction of Wells Road and Broadwalk, proceed parallel with and then behind Knowle cricket ground along Kingshill Road. Cross Greenleaze, and after 200 yards turn left onto a tarmac path down to a footpath across Broadfield Road and Hill Crescent onto Ponsford Road. Turn left to meet Wells Road. Turn right and cross to your left first set of traffic lights to walk along Wootton Park and Callington Road path. Walk to underpass near superstore. Through underpass bear left onto second footpath to follow Callington Road again. As the road starts to climb, turn left into Runnymead Avenue and cross the pedestrian bridge. After the footbridge, double back along the shops and find a walkway between two of the shops along a fenced lane, bearing left to Glenarm Walk. Cross over to Brislington church.

The White Hart **A** in Brislington village became a coaching inn on the Bath-Bristol Road in 1738 and was also the venue for bare-knuckle boxing and church vestry meetings, though one hopes not at the same time. (A White Hart was adopted by Richard II as his emblem in 1390.) The pub served at one time as Brislington's first post office. In what used to be an open meadow behind it was the village green. Pilgrims to the chapel and holy well in St Anne's wood would meet between here and the adjoining Kenneth Road.

A parish poor house was built here in 1722. It consisted of six rooms on each of the two storeys. Inmates were set to work. The churchwardens, one of them George Weare whose silver paten, given to the church in 1778, is still in use every Sunday, purchased a 'pull of old rope' for picking into oakum by these unfortunates.

In St Luke's churchyard **B** is the gravestone of Thomas Newman, said to have died in 1542 aged 153. 'To perpetuate the great age of the deceased', it was recarved in 1771. The church of Bridlington in Yorkshire also records the death of a Thomas Newman who died at 153. In 1819, the vicar was William Conybeare, the geologist who was the first man to describe the ichthyosaurus.

In 1828, two doctors were caught in the graveyard, equipped with 'a shovel, a sack and a powerful turn-screw upon a novel construction, a packing needle and a coil of rope'. They were fined £6 for grave robbing, but three weeks later the same magistrate proposed one of them, Dr Wallis who founded the anatomy school, to be physician to the Infirmary.

A chapel on this site was built in 1308 for the benefit of pilgrims from Keynsham Abbey and the holy well at St Anne's.

Opposite the church originally stood a fifteenth century pilgrims' hostel where Henry VII is said to have rested. John Leland, the sixteenth century English antiquary, wrote, 'On the morne when the King had dined he rode on a pilgrimage to St Anne in the beautiful little wood at Brislington'.

Exit into Church Hill and follow the stone wall on your left hand side, reaching a T-junction. Turn right at Hill Street till you pass a cemetery ground on the left.

Church Hill House **C** was built in the Palladian style early in the eighteenth century. Originally it was part of Brislington Hill House estate. From 1820-1850s it was a boarding school for 'sons of gentlemen' known as the CHH Academy. From 1896 to 1981 it was St Luke's vicarage. Pevsner described it as 'a specially pretty early Georgian house ... the middle window on the first floor is of the Venetian type'. It's now a private house.

Another Church Hill House and Keeper's Cottage are notable places remaining on the estate. Brislington House, late eighteenth century, was developed as a lunatic asylum by Dr Fox, the famous mad doctor, enlightened for his time, who was consulted in the case of George III.

Continue in a straight line through the park, via gate and diagonally across the next field to exit over the stile onto Bonville Road. Turn left and just past Devon Road, take footpath via a stile across a meadow, following the overhead power lines to a stile, then go along the fenced footpath with allotments on the left. Exit on to School Road, cross over to the Rock following pavement and path past Millbank Close. Continue past stone walls into the Rock cul-de-sac. Turn left onto tarmac path that crosses a stream. Bear right slightly uphill and turn right behind the cottage gardens onto a green space. In the dip of Allison Road, cross over into Nightingale Valley on right hand side. Follow Riverside Path for a quarter of a mile until you turn right where a stone bridge crosses the river. Keep the stream on your left hand side as footpath bears right and uphill. Go through a metal gate where tarmac path bears sharp left and follows backs of houses with paddocks on the right hand side. At the end past garages turn right in front of houses and along to steps rising to the road. Alternatively, in dry months, take path through the metal gate mentioned above, and up along a green path with paddocks on your left hand side, allotments emerging to your right. Reaching the lane, turn left onto Latimer Close. Follow left hand path or straight ahead to Birchwood Road.

On the lane you will find well established allotments which remain the only council plots allowing the raising of chickens. Also here are prefabricated houses dating back to the war which have proved their worth by attracting private owners.

Cross Birchwood Road to Jersey Avenue. After 20 yards turn left to follow back lane (ignoring crossing lanes) past old persons' housing, to the end. Turn left down to a T-junction with Eastwood Road/Crescent and Wyndham Crescent to the right and left respectively. Follow Wyndham Crescent until at a bend in the road a tarmac lane on left leads you into Eastwood Farm yard. Before the yard entrance, follow the leafy path that leads off to the right to join the Eastwood Farm Park roadway. (The roadway could be reached by walking to the end of Wyndham Crescent. Turn left into Whitmore Crescent through public entrance into park.)

The 56 acres of Eastwood Farm Open Space and Nature Reserve **D** is managed for nature conservation and leisure by Bristol City Council with the support of the Countryside Agency. It is a valuable haven for wildlife. Many different plants, birds, and animals can be found in the woodland, water meadows and other habitats here. Follow the nature trail and see how much of this rich variety you can find.

The seventeenth century farmhouse (Grade II listed) still stands, approached from a path off Wyndham Crescent. It has fine moulded plaster ceilings, a carved stone fireplace and a carved oak staircase.

*Along the roadway after about 50 yards, opposite farm garden, take the stepped path down and turn left along green path that leads to the riverside, nature reserve and picnic sites, then on to the tea gardens down river **E**. The tea garden is reached by walking uphill along a gravel path, through a stile to the garden entrance.*

As a traditional destination for Bristolians in search of rustic jollification, Beese's Tea Garden ranks with New Passage Hotel, the Salutation and the Lamplighters. Opened in 1846 it was originally owned by a Mr Plumton, but the name of Mother Beese stuck. Many boat trips called there and it was served by ferry from St George.

An oral history of Hanham records that this stretch of river was popular with children between the wars because of the good chance of seeing a drowned corpse recovered.

From tea gardens near gateway take path ahead, uphill through the woods past a wooden bungalow. The path rises to steps and divides. For the No 36 bus back to Knowle, carry on to top of steps. Turn right along Eastwood Road, and Birchwood Road to St Anne's Park Road. For the No 1 bus to the centre, at top of first flight of steps turn left along wide footpath leading to open space and playgrounds. Cross to exit at footpath sign via back lane to reach Broomhill Road. Cross over to public house and bus stop beyond. Alternatively, from exit gate of tea gardens a gravel track leads up to the park exit at Wyndham Crescent.

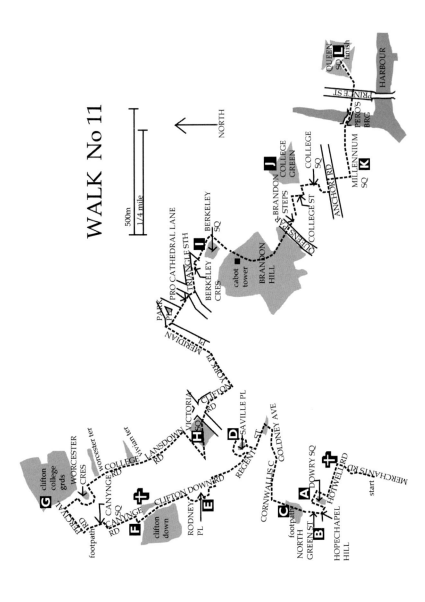

WALK No 11

CLIFTON SQUARES

Description: *This walk covers the squares of Hotwells, Clifton and Central Bristol referring to the major and minor celebrities who have lived in them.*
Length: *3·4 miles.*
Refreshments: *Many pubs and cafés en route.*
Transport: *Bus no 57 (Mon-Fri), country buses and the harbour ferry link the beginning and end of the linear walk. To cut it short, take 8/9 from Clifton or one of the many services up Park Street.*

On alighting from the bus on Merchants Road, Hotwells (N.B. there is another road of the same name in Clifton) turn left towards the church, cross the road and go left to Dowry Square. Walk round the square noting the plaque in the top left hand corner.

Dowry Square **A** probably has the strangest associations of any street in Bristol, deserving a place in the affections of literary types, drinkers, dentists and drug addicts. Here early in 1812 the economic migrant Jacob Schweppe opened his fizz factory. Here Dr Thomas Beddoes ran his clinic, attempting to cure consumption by introducing cows into the patients' bedrooms. He and his assistant Humphrey Davy did much for the gaiety of nations by producing nitrous oxide, popular amongst the intelligentsia as a recreational drug. Another assistant, Peter Roget, compiled the Thesaurus.

Beddoes son, also Thomas Lovell, is Bristol's greatest poet and certainly one of the most distinctive poets in the literature, albeit distinctively morbid and macabre. Like his father, whom the local library barred as 'not Blue enough', he was a political radical which got him into trouble in Switzerland and caused him to be expelled by 'the ingenious jackanapes of Bavaria'. He made several attempts at suicide, losing a leg in the process, and finally succeeded in 1849, using curare. There is no kudos in self-slaughter at the age of forty-five so he never achieved the stereotypical

fame of Chatterton. His best remembered poem is the anthologised *Dream Pedlary*: 'If there were dreams to sell, what would you buy? Some cost a passing bell; some a light sigh'. His gothic gifts are displayed in his plays, notably *Death's Jest Book*. Compare this with the gimcrack archaism of Chatterton:

'Squats on a toad-stool under a tree
A bodiless child full of life in the gloom
Crying with frog voice
What shall I be?
What shall I be? Shall I creep to the egg?
That's cracking asunder yonder by Nile,
And with eighteen toes,
And a snuff taking nose
Make an Egyptian crocodile?'

A lighter poet of the gruesome and grotesque, the Revd Richard Harris Barham of the *Ingoldsby Legends* stayed in the square seeking and failing to find health. His last work was written here.

Leave the Square and turn right up Hopechapel Hill, right into North Green Street and either make a detour left along the footpath beside the Polygon Gardens leading to Hope Chapel and turn right up the Hill to Hope Square or go straight on up the path to Cornwallis Crescent, turn right to Goldney Avenue and left on the footpath to Regent Street.

Many developments in Clifton bankrupted the speculator. Hope Square **B**, named for a Lady, not a virtue, is one example. Up the hill (a later development as Hotwells was fashionable before Clifton), Cornwallis Crescent **C** took so long to complete that the path you use was established across its line. This delay had far-reaching effects. The architect, Francis Greenway, whose firm bought the unfinished buildings as a speculation, was driven to forgery. His death sentence was commuted to transportation and he became the Father of Australian Architecture.

Note the plaque at No 30 Cornwallis Crescent to the Winkworth sisters, translators of German poetry who were concerned with female education and decent housing for the poor.

Cross Regent Street and walk round Saville Place. (The alley at the top right hand corner provides a short cut to Victoria Square should you wish to shorten the walk.)

In Saville Place **D** lived E.H. Young, novelist of the shabby genteel; she has been rediscovered and reprinted by Virago.

*Turn right along Regent Street and Clifton Down Road, cross over at zebra crossing and continue right to Rodney Place **E** on your left.*

Admiral Rodney was especially popular in the city because he secured British control of Jamaica, where many Bristolians had investments. Here there is yet another plaque to Dr Beddoes and one to his pupil Radical Jack Lambton, Earl of Durham. '£40,000 a year' he said was 'a moderate income such a one as a man might jog on with.' Despite this, he was a fervent supporter of the Reform Bill. Recalled from the Governorship of Canada for exceeding his constitutional powers in settling a rebellion - his nickname was 'the Dictator' - he wrote, or at least signed the Durham Report which staved off a Canadian Revolution on the American model and set the liberal pattern for the white dominions of the British Empire.

Return to Clifton Down Road, cross over mini-roundabout in front of Christ Church and head for the cottages beyond the Church.

Briefly, Walter Savage Landor lived at Penrose Cottage **F** where Southey visited him. His outrageous temper made residence in England difficult. On one occasion, he threw his cook out of the window breaking his arm. Landor regretted the action when he remembered the violets were underneath that window.

Follow Canynge Road to Canynge Square. Return to Canynge Road and follow to Percival Road right.

Clifton College **G** was the first public school of the modern foundations, training the children of the middle classes to bear the lucrative burden of Empire. John Percival, after whom the road was named, was its first headmaster.

Clifton College Close, before you, has its place in the dubious statistical annals of cricket: A.J. Collins, 628 not out in a very protracted house match. It is also the setting of Newbolt's *Vitaï Lampada*: The Torch of Life, the place where there was a breathless hush, a bumping pitch and a blinding light. Other men of letters associated with Clifton College are Quiller-Couch and T.E. Brown, the Manx poet ('a garden is a lovesome thing, God wot'), a retired housemaster who died on a visit to the school and was buried at Redland Chapel.

Douglas Haig has a statue overlooking the Close. A more useful old boy was Leslie Hore-Belisha who brought an ungrateful nation such unglamorous innovations as the driving test, the Highway Code and the eponymous beacon. He also sought to reform and democratise the Army.

At 8 College Road, then 34 Worcester Lawn, Dr George Spear Thompson organised the first Bristol demonstration of the telephone at a scientific soirée on 4th October 1877. Alexander Graham Bell came from London at short notice to explain the gadget and its potential uses. To demonstrate, someone sang a line of 'God save the Queen' at the Mayoress. A young man who helped at the demonstration, in 1922, as Lord Mayor himself, took part in a test wireless transmission between Marconi House in London and Bristol.

Turn along College Road, follow Worcester Crescent round and continue along College Road. Cross Clifton Park into Lansdown Road, noting Worcester Terrace and Vyvyan Terrace on the way to Victoria Square ◼. *Walk anti-clockwise round the square.*

There is a plaque to John Addington Symonds, critic, poet and (monumental) art historian. The real hero of Victoria Square, however, has no plaque, though he does have a place in legal textbooks. *R v Matthias* is still cited when the 'usual accompaniment of a foot passenger' is under consideration. William Matthias was nicknamed 'General' because of his long drawn campaigns against the Corporation and the Merchant Venturers Society. One of these concerned Boyce's Avenue, through the arch in the corner of the Square. Matthias said it was public footpath; the Merchant Venturers, the developers, said it was a public carriageway. The disagreement lasted a quarter of a century and the developers hired navvies to break down Matthias's barricades. In 1861 when he turned back a woman with a perambulator by pushing her on the shoulder, the Corporation encouraged a prosecution for assault.

The vehicle stopped by Mr Matthias being a perambulator - then a novel invention - no precedents could be adduced, and there was much legal contention as to the right of such a carriage to pass along footpaths. The absurd female fashion of wearing crinoline, an article which had just swollen to extreme monstrosity, was also amusingly introduced. Mr Matthias's counsel asked if a lady whose dress spread the entire width of the path was to be turned back by a perambulator, upon which Mr Justice Byles thought that a baby's carriage would not be half so formidable an obstruction as the meeting of one lady with another. Eventually the jury disagreed and was discharged but it had been decided that legally a pram is not a carriage. In the end Matthias won and a supporter wrote an acrostic.

William the Conqueror! Art thou righted now?
In spite of Civic spite or Civic row:
Leonidas of Clifton's Pass of Boyce!
Let Clifton in such British pluck rejoice.
In many a gallant fight, 'tis thine to boast
A host against thee - but thyself a host;
Majestic still, thou stoodst guarding thy rightful Post;

Might *versus* Right, good General! Was't not so?
And thou seemd'st 'chosen' first to bear the blow.
Tongues rave against thee, as a perfect bore;
The Scribbling tribe abused thee more and more;
Horsemen oft trespassed on thy Right of Way;
In Law Courts too they sued, costs made thee pay;
And Nursemaids charged thee with uncourteous hustle;
Still hast thou vanquish'd all, spite of this boisterous bustle.

Matthias's campaigning came to a sad end In 1873, at the age of 92, he was imprisoned for six months for disobeying a court order to restore a road he had dug up.

In Boyce's Avenue itself worked Edwin Bailey, a cobbler. In 1871, he raped a maid sent to collect a pair of boots. When the girl gave birth, he arranged to have her child dosed with Steadman's Settling Powders, laced with strychnine rat poison.

The house next to the arch in Victoria Square has a plaque to W.G. Grace, the snobbish, unsporting but phenomenal cricketer.

From the archway, take the path across the Square, cross Merchants Road. Avoid the temptations of the Fosseway and Church Walk and follow Clifton Road. Turn left along York Place to Park Place. Leave by Pro Cathedral Lane on the right. Cross to look at Upper Berkeley Place, Turn right up Triangle South, right up steps to Berkeley Crescent and follow round to Berkeley Square. Go clockwise round the square.

At No 23 ∎, lived John McAdam, surveyor to the Bristol Turnpike Trust, who shaped the modern world by inventing a cheap way to make light roads.

Note the remains of Bristol's replica High Cross in the garden of the square. The original was removed as a traffic obstruction in the eighteenth century and sold as a garden ornament. The replica stood on College Green. Amateurs of street names should collect There and Back Again Lane. Except for the name it is of no interest whatsoever.

(To cut the walk short leave by bottom left hand corner. Bus stops for the Centre are on the left.) Leave Berkeley Square by the top left hand corner and turn into Brandon Hill, take path down to bottom, turn right and left down Brandon steps, cross the car park right up College Street, to College Green ◨.

The Cathedral was converted from a Norman abbey by Henry VIII. The building was not finished until the nineteenth century. Next to it stood the Bishop's Palace until it was burnt down in the riots of 1831. On College Green, note the Art Deco House. Relish the delightful lack of traffic in front of the Cathedral. A few years ago an enterprising Council closed the road.

Through the Norman arch beyond the Library, go round College Square, formerly Lower College Green to the pedestrian crossing, then left to Millennium Square ◧. Leave by bottom left hand corner for the horned bridge to Queen Square.

Queen Square ◧, was a fashionable development in the early eighteenth century. Much of it was burnt down in 1831 during the famous 'Reform' riot. A few drunken rioters were enveloped in boiling lead. 130 people were killed or wounded as the cavalry restored order. During the nineteenth century a railway embankment and a central station were proposed. In 1939 the Corporation did actually build a dual carriageway across the middle which has now been closed and dug up by a more enlightened administration.

Richard Bright, best known for the kidney disease named after him, is commemorated by a plaque. He also wrote a book of Hungarian travels, informative about gypsies.

Thaddeus Kosciuszko, the Polish Patriot, passed through Bristol in 1797 on his way to the United States after defeat by the Russian Empire. Earlier in his career, he had fought in the American War of Independence on the side of the colonists, helping win the battle of Saratoga. He was granted land in Ohio which he left in his will for the education of black Americans. A national park and the highest peak in Australia are named after him, and, for good measure, the birthplace of Oprah Winfrey.

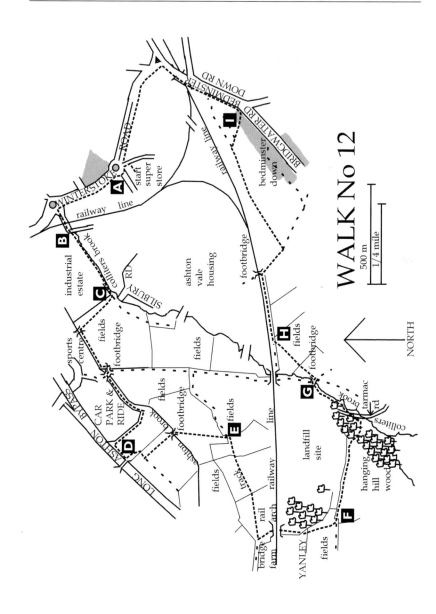

WALK No 12

500 m
1/4 mile

NORTH

YANLEY

Description: *The rural fringe and views from Bedminster Down.*
Length: *4 miles.*
Refreshments: *Pubs at end.*
Transport: *24, 25, 520 to the Robins, Winterstoke Road.*

From the Robins **A**, *turn left down Winterstoke Road. Immediately after Brunel Ford, turn left on to Barons Close. Keep to right hand side of road. At end of road cross railway line on to path (Colliter's Brook on left).*

An undistinguished cigar factory on the left is the last working reminder of the industry which made such a notable impact on the architecture of this side of Bristol.

The recreation ground on the opposite side of Winterstoke Road is the site of Gore's Marsh pit. There were several collieries and associated industries - iron rolling mills, brickworks - hereabouts. Gore is a personal name: the coal-owner's family lived at Barrow Court. In the mid-eighteenth century, when turnpike toll houses, unpopular with farmers and colliers alike, though coal carts were exempt, were being destroyed by riotous mobs, there is an entry in Mr Gore's account book 'To Mr Hardwick, for cutting down the turnpikes, £10'.

The railway **B** was originally built to serve a Portishead dock scheme intended to increase the value of Bristol Corporation's estate there. Lovers of the picturesque were concerned about the impact of a railway line under Leigh Woods along the bank of the Avon, but a promoter of the scheme assured them that 'no better security could be founded for the preservation of the beauty of the woods than the construction of the railway, as it would put a stop to the quarrying and blasting which had so much damaged them'. It didn't. The line has recently been re-opened to carry freight from Portbury Dock. As part of the solution to Bristol's transport problems, it is to be hoped that it will be re-opened also for passengers, and indeed that all of the City's rail network will be intelligently exploited.

At end **C** *(Silbury Road to left) turn right into field. The obvious path heading for the church tower is not actually a right of way. Strictly, you should follow the field boundaries anti-clockwise to the second footbridge. Cross bridge. Turn left and skirt round fence (Park & Ride on right): warning - muddy! Follow footpath by fence next to Long Ashton by-pass* **D***.*

The church tower on the skyline is Dundry. The fifteenth century tower, much grander than its church, was commissioned by Bristol merchants, perhaps to welcome their ships returning. A natural transport corridor, Ashton Vale demonstrates that for better or worse Transportation is Civilisation. There are old turnpike roads, the main railway to the South West, car-based ribbon development at Long Ashton, the obtrusive and dangerous three-lane bypass which this made necessary and finally the tarmac wasteland of a Park & Ride, the City's cheap and cheerless substitute for a decent public transport system.

Once, fashionable visitors to the Hotwells Spa would cross Rownham Ferry and stroll to Ashton to eat strawberries and cream.

At clearing, go through gate and turn left on to path. Follow path keeping to left hand side, Keep straight on towards bridge and cross Ashton Brook. Fork right: barbed wire fence on right. Continue on this line across field, to a new plantation, part of the Forest of Avon Community Forest. Here there may be a temporary fence with a stile. Cross it and follow path to the hedge **E***. There should be another stile hidden in it, otherwise go through the metal gate. Turn right, keep along hedge. After about 30 yards, at clearing, turn right onto stony path. Go through glade and two fields. Just after end of second field (raised section of A370 ahead) turn left. Pass under railway arch. Path goes round to right. Cross stile and turn left. Keep to left of field, cross stile and ascend hill* **F***.*

The view from the top, across the rubbish tip to the old city, the tower blocks, the Suspension Bridge and Clifton provokes historical reflection and allegorical interpretation. As you move on, note the interesting building on the skyline which was built as offices for the Central Electricity Generating Board.

At top of hill cross stile into field. Walk along the bottom of field. At edge of woods, cross waymarked stile under the spindle tree and descend to tarmac road (leads to landfill site). Turn left. After 30 yards turn right over stile. Ignore the bridge and walk between the pool (on left) and Colliter's Brook (on right). Cross the second bridge **G** *and turn left along the bottom of the field parallel with the brook. Then bear right, closing with the railway line. Ignore the arch under the line and climb to a metal barrier* **H**. *Climb this gate-like iron bar and follow the narrow path by the railway. (A more adventurous route ignores the second bridge,*

keeps Colliter's brook on the right as far as the railway, and turns right over stepping stones to pick up the path to the metal barrier.) Path descends slightly. At junction (railway bridge to left) turn right and climb narrow path. As path levels out into clearing turn left into field. Follow path across field (allotments on right). At end of field turn right, climbing to a small glade by the side of Bridgwater Road ■. Walk up to, and join, Bridgwater Road which descends into Bedminster Down Road. At bottom both The Miners' Arms and The Plough await.

In 1740, a soldier was hanged in chains on Bedminster Down for atrocious robberies at Bedminster and Brislington, a burglary in the city and the theft of twenty-one sheep in the southern suburbs. His accomplice was gibbeted on Brislington Common. There were thousands of spectators.

It is possible to end the walk here and return to the centre by bus (52 or 75). The train service from Parson Street is deplorable. To return to the starting point on Winterstoke Road, cross Bedminster Down Road into Winterstoke Road and keep to left, passing HMS Flying Fox on left.

Perhaps the name of South Liberty Lane derives ultimately from the time when Bedminster lay outside the jurisdiction of the City magistrates, though South Liberty was a colliery name. (Curiously, Bristol Castle itself was also outside the law from 1373, when Bristol became a County, to 1629. Technically, it was still part of Gloucestershire whose authorities could not care less that its surroundings swarmed with 'robbers, malefactors and inordinate livers'.)

HMS Flying Fox perpetuates the name of the ship that used to be moored for naval reserve training in the Float by Hotwell Road.

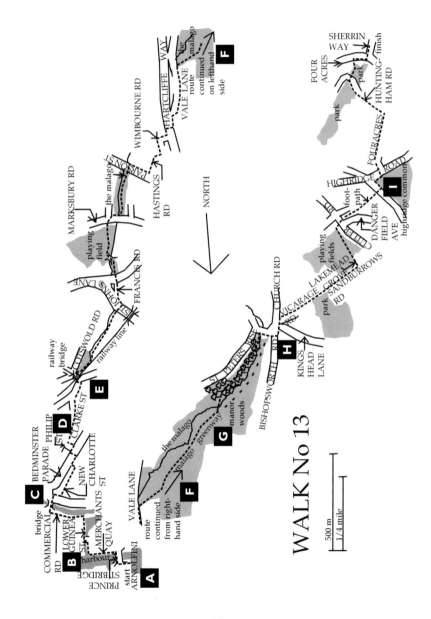

WALK No 13

500 m

1/4 mile

MALAGO GREENWAY

Description: *This walk from the City Centre to Bishopsworth follows the River Malago. It is based on the Malago Greenway, which provides a cycle route between the City Centre and Hartcliffe and is signed by a disc with a white leaf on a green background. A map of the 1998 edition of the Malago Greenway is available in public libraries and is helpful to walkers. However, explorers of Bristol Backs will find that our route which starts from Prince Street is more tranquil than the Gaol Ferry Bridge/Dean Lane route.*

Length: *4½ miles.*

Refreshments: *Bedminster Parade and Windmill Hill City Farm.*

Transport: *Bus no 75 serves Sherrin Way and Bishopsworth Library. No 77 serves Bishopsworth Library. Both stop on the Centre a few hundred yards from the start of the walk.*

In 1987 Bristol City Council's Planning Department aimed to create a greenway and also initiate a range of environmental improvements such as clearing the river, new planting, seating and children's play areas (see 1990 leaflet). As an urban walking and cycling route to Bishopsworth, it is very successful. It is also a reminder of the importance of public services.

Start at the Arnolfini Art Gallery, Narrow Quay **A**. *Turn left to the Prince Street road bridge and cross it. Turn left along Merchant Quay, cross the footbridge* **B** *and walk beside Bathurst Basin to Commercial Road.*

Before the Cut was built, Trin Mills, on the site of Bathurst Basin was the confluence of the Malago and the Avon. Opposite the footbridge is the entrance to the railway tunnel under St Mary Redcliffe. Given the inconvenient situation of Temple Meads, the closure of this line towards the centre can only be described as the waste of an asset. Unfortunately, it is said, the tunnel cannot be re-opened because the pile foundations of modern buildings obstruct it. Note the characteristic 'Bristol Byzantine' warehouse with ogee window-heads preserved on the west side.

Beside the basin on the east side is the General Hospital, set up in the nineteenth century when the Infirmary was inadequate. There was rivalry, articulated by party and sect. At the Tory, Church Infirmary one hoped for a Sovereign Remedy, at the Liberal, Dissenting General, for a Radical Cure.

Turn left to Bedminster Bridge, cross it, turn right on Coronation Road and left along New Charlotte Street with ASDA car park on right. Turn left past the Library and cross Bedminster Parade to Philip Street to your right.

At the corner of Coronation Road stands Zion Chapel **C** now occupied by Bristol's Housing Services. In 1773, John Hare, a poor young man from Taunton, seeking his fortune in Bristol, stopped for a rest on the outskirts of the city. When he woke, he was so struck by the beauty of the spot he thought he would like to build a house of prayer there. After about fifty six years, having grown wealthy by the manufacture of floor cloth, he did indeed erect a chapel. A few years later, following dissent among the dissenters, the trustees refused him a pew.

This is an opportunity to visit Bedminster Library and investigate the Local Studies section which is well stocked with local history (closed on Wednesdays).

This is also an opportunity to visit Windmill Hill City Farm which was set up in 1976 as a result of demands by local residents that derelict land in this area of inner-city Bristol be used. The City Farm **D** clearly achieves its aim of serving the community. There is a range of activities for children of all ages, plus self-help groups, a Senior Citizen group and the 'Memories of Bedminster' Group. Local people can get involved in the farm and community gardens in various ways. Judging by the café at lunchtime, there's a healthy local population of under fives. More than 130,000 people a year visit the Farm (closed on Mondays).

Just before the City Farm, turn right off Philip Street into Clarke Street. As a through road for cars, this has been severed, but pedestrians can follow a footpath between the two sections. Do not follow the ditch, actually the Malago itself, round to the right, but keep straight on between the car park and some waste land. From the end of Clarke Street, keep straight on to visit the GreenHouse **E**. *Walk up the steps of this tree-shrouded building which is open during office hours.*

The History of the GreenHouse is the title of an attractive leaflet which is worth picking up. The development of this area is shown on a timeline from a water mill on the Malago in 600 AD to a hospital for pilgrims in East Street up until it was home to miners and small industries.

The GreenHouse is the headquarters of the Federation of City Farms and Community Gardens. The leaflet describes it as a 'unique, purpose-built community building constructed of wood with a wildflower meadow for a roof'. The GreenHouse, like Bristol's other environmental icon, the CREATE Centre, is sometimes open to the public. The contrast of this elegant building and the outside world is dramatic. In 1996, Bristol women were invited to write poems, plays or songs about the environment. They were auditioned at the GreenHouse by a women who was working on

Local Agenda 21 (Agenda 21 aims to improve the environment). The experience inspired Debbie Smith, from nearby Knowle West, to write this poem:

    Thought I'd buy them friendly products
    The ones that don't harm the earth
    So I went off to the supermarket
    For to buy a fivers worth.
    Eco powder to do the wash
    Friendly liquid to scrub the dishes clean
    All in highly degradable packaging -
    It felt good to go green.
    Went to the checkout
    Prepared to pay my bit.
    Can't believe the price they asked.
    Costs the earth to go green - dunnit?

Just before the GreenHouse, walk under the railway bridge. Admire the mural on the left, then cross the road onto a grassy area and follow the Malago Greenway to St John's Lane.

A notice board on a pole warns that you are being watched by CCTV. A children's play area was created on the open space as planned, but it was vandalised and removed in 2000.

Cross at the lights on your left and walk up Francis Road. Cross the road on the pelican crossing and continue along the path to Marksbury Road.

Once again you can see the plans of 1987 in ruins. The children's play area was built and featured in the 1990 version of the Malago Greenway leaflet. In the late 1990s a workman was employed more or less full time to mend the play equipment, which was frequently destroyed and has now been removed. The skeleton of a netball/basketball pitch remains without any posts. It is still used in summer evenings by young people who have no other recreational facilities.

Look right for the Malago sign and follow the path to Parson Street. Turn right, then left into Hastings Road leading through an attractive new housing estate. At Hartcliffe Way, take the pedestrian crossing to your left.

This is an opportunity to celebrate people power. The 1990 version of the Malago Greenway project promised 'light controlled crossings' where necessary. Traffic increased but there was no controlled crossing on Hartcliffe Way (A4174). Knowing how dangerous it was to cross this busy road, the Ramblers leader on the mid-week walk in February 1997 prepared a traffic-calming walking stick decorated with a fluorescent strip. Eighteen well-wrapped and well-equipped Ramblers waited at the roadside as the traffic shot past. Eventually a double-decker bus stopped and the Ramblers crossed safely. Thanks to letters and petitions to Bristol City Council, a pelican crossing was installed the following year.

Walk along Vale Lane and through the entrance to a spacious grassy area on the right **F**. *Follow the tarmac path.*

The entrance to this section of the Greenway is the result of consultation. Bristol City Council invited people to comment on their design in 1996. The completed work consists of a sturdy stone wall and some wooden planks which unfortunately are not wide enough to create a shelter. It amazes me that there was money for an ornate entrance and yet no money to supply recreational facilities on this vast prairie.

Walk on the grass or follow the tarmac path until you reach a concrete structure, which is the Malago Flood Relief Scheme **G**. *You now have a choice. The tarmac route to the right of the stream leads to Bishopsworth. But if you have strong shoes and enjoy walking with the feel of earth beneath your feet, take the path on the left hand side into Manor Woods and enjoy a tranquil stroll to Bishopsworth. All the paths through the wood come out to the same place.*

By now you will have decided that the Malago is more like a ditch than a river. But that's because you don't know its ferocious past. The Bristol

City Council Malago Greenway leaflet gives background details. The Malago is formed by the various streams which drain the northern slopes of Dundry Hill. It then runs through South Bristol before joining the River Avon at Coronation Road. In the early part of the last century, the Malago provided both drinking water and recreational facilities for the people of South Bristol.

But the Malago could also be dangerous. Heavy rain on Dundry turned the stream into a raging torrent which claimed many lives and flooded large areas of Bedminster and Southville. Bishopsworth also suffered as the river became 20 feet deep and the ground floors of nearby houses were flooded. Following the 1968 floods, a massive new stormwater tunnel was built which now diverts the stream's flow to the Avon at the bottom of Rownham Hill.

Manor Woods provides a tranquil walking route. The path is high above the stream which allows you to look down on an imposing incline of trees. There's a range of flowers with primrose and violets in March, cow parsley, wild garlic and buttercups in May and dandelions, daises and wild strawberries in June. Cross the flat stone slabs and watch out for moorhens and herons. I chatted to a group of teenagers before entering the woods and was warned of danger! I frightened a few birds. Twigs snapped under my feet and broke the silence. It was autumn and a red leaf spiralled slowly to my feet.

Walk out of the woods and up the lane past the public lavatories then turn right for Bishopsworth Library (closed Wednesdays) ▐. *The walk can be cut short here.*

The Malago Valley Conservation Group produces an attractively illustrated guide to Manor Woods. The Malago Society - the local history society for south-west Bristol - produces a beautifully illustrated Bishopsworth Village Trail which starts from the library.

The Malago Valley Conservation Group makes valiant efforts to create an awareness and a pride in the locality. But they have a problem which is clear to anyone who walks the Greenway. The route is boarded by spacious swathes of grass which must delight dog owners but provides no physical or mental challenges. There are no goal posts, no basketball or football pitches, no play areas and no stimulus.

Outside Bishopsworth Library is an enormous board with the word **OPEN** printed on it. The evolution of this sign is as follows: library built with large windows; large windows allow sunlight to dazzle library users; large windows replaced by dark windows; dark windows give the appearance of locked building. Walk into the library and ask for nature and historic trails.

Cross Bishopsworth Road and Kings Head Lane. Follow Vicarage Road, on the right, and Sandburrows Road then take Lakemead Grove on the left and continue straight on over the playing field. Turn right. Cross Cutler Road to the unsigned path by the electricity substation. It leads between the gardens of Dangerfield Road and Wyatt Avenue. When it comes out at a turning circle with a silver birch, turn left through the gap in the hedge with view of Dundry Church on the skyline ■. Go left and right to skirt Highridge Common and take the left turn; Four Acres. At Huntingham Road turn left and follow the road to the park. Turn right into the park and follow the tarmac path to the left of the colourful building which is Withywood Area Office. Turn right on Four Acres and cross to Sherrin Way. Here the walk ends at the bus stop, unless you care to follow paths on the OS map over the city boundary to Dundry.

WALK No 14

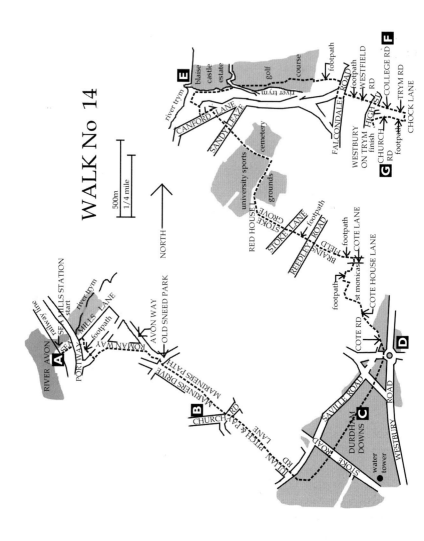

AVON AND TRYM

Description: *This walk embraces a variety of urban landscape, ranging from the up-market houses of Sneyd Park, via the wide-open Downs and through hidden paths to historic Westbury village.*

Length: *4¾ miles*

Refreshments: *There are two refreshment caravans on the Downs, one by the water tower and one just before the White Tree roundabout. In Westbury village there are several pubs and cafés.*

Transport: *The walk starts at Sea Mills station on the Severn Beach line. At the end of the walk in Westbury on Trym, there are numerous bus routes, including the hourly 52 service back to Sea Mills station and buses (1 and 55) to Clifton Down station to rejoin the Severn Beach line. Intermediately, on the Downs there are numerous bus routes serving the top of Blackboy Hill and the White Tree roundabout.*

Start at Sea Mills station.

The railway at Sea Mills **A** was opened to passengers as the Clifton Extension Railway in 1885 to provide access to the newly completed Avonmouth Docks.

On arrival at Sea Mills station and before starting the walk proper it is worth crossing the railway, using the path at the end of the platform to reach the river Avon.

There are wide views here and if it is approaching high tide boats may be seen on their way to or from the Bristol City Docks. Regrettably there is no commercial shipping now, although occasional naval craft and the Channel passenger ships 'Balmoral' and 'Waverley' call. At low tide the mud flats attract waders and seabirds. Also to be seen are the old signal stations, now incorporated into houses, which used to warn ships of other traffic and informed the City dockmaster about incoming vessels.

Recross the railway and walk up Sea Mills Lane.

On the left is the mouth of the river Trym which is the site of the Roman port of Abona, and which was made into a small dock in 1712, before the Floating Harbour was built. Remains of the eighteenth century works can be seen. Too far from the city, with poor road links, it was not popular with merchants. Later it was used by privateers and whalers.

After passing under the Portway viaduct, turn right into a road labelled 'Private Road', the path passing between the flats and garages. Turn left along Roman Way to Avon Way. Turn right and after about 100 metres, take a short path through the bushes on the right to reach Old Sneed Park. Opposite the picturesque thatched cottage (originally the lodge of Sneyd Park) take the ancient Mariners Path. which runs parallel to Mariners Drive.

This area has many opulent houses, and we pass by St Mary Magdalene church **B**, built in 1850 by the Bristol architect John Norton, in the

Victorian Gothic style which is worth a visit. The path is following the probable line of the Roman Road to Sea Mills.

The path continues climbing all the way and crossing a metalled road, to become Pitch and Pay Lane. Then it joins Julian Road and so leads onto the Downs.

Pitch and Pay Lane purports to get its name from times of plague, when country people were reluctant to enter the city and business was conducted by tossing goods across a barrier, with the money being thrown back the other way. (Ordinarily, the phrase means to pay cash down, on the nail.)

On the Downs, ignore the tarmacked path and strike off left across the grass along the centre of the Downs, keeping well left of the water tower.

The Downs **C** are one of Bristol's finest assets, but by the middle of the nineteenth century, they were threatened by creeping development, and were only saved by the Downs Act passed in 1861.

In 1850, the Council had discussed the process by which, on the sheep walks 'a few rails were put up, ostensibly to prevent the sheep from wandering. These soon gave way to iron stanchions; by-and-by a wall was built, and then houses were erected. Opposite these houses small shrubs were planted, and under pretence of protecting them, posts were put up. Within a few years the posts were pulled down and regular plantations formed.' One councillor expressed fears that they would eventually terminate in the enclosure of Clifton Down.

When Alderman Pinney advised the purchase of the Downs, an eccentric councillor (he regularly warned the Council that Brandon Hill was a dormant volcano that would fill up the Floating Harbour one day) advanced a familiar argument. He protested against the Council interfering with the property of others. 'If the Merchants Society,' he said, 'chose to build upon Clifton Down, they would be dealing with their own property, and the Council had no more right to intervene than to pull down Badminton House.' In the following August, the lords of the manor of Henbury, who included Sir Greville Smyth, 'doing what they liked with their own,' sold the St John's school site. In 1856 someone built a cottage in one of the five quarries which were then being worked in various parts of the Downs. This step excited so much indignation, however, that the building was forthwith removed.

In the course of the following year, the Corporation bought a property with rights of common and appointed a committee to negotiate with the landowners. Although the Merchant Venturers Society refused to sell their rights to Clifton Down, it was willing to see the public assured of the free enjoyment of the open space. The lords of Henbury Manor sold their rights on Durdham, including the quarries. An Act of Parliament legalising the settlement received the royal assent a year later. The whole deal, including parliamentary expenses, cost £16,296. For this, the public acquired a right of perpetual enjoyment over 442 acres, 230 acres of which belong to Clifton Down and 212 to that of Durdham.

Unfortunately, Bristol City Council, which is supposed to enforce the act in conjunction with the Merchant Venturers Society, sometimes has other ideas. Even in 1862, just after the Downs Act was passed, the Downs Committee agreed to a controversial road scheme. Mr Baker wanted a road to serve his new development at Sneyd Park and was paid £550 to construct it, but owing to the disapproval expressed by the citizens, the turf was ordered to be replaced and he not merely retained the contract price, but got £200 more for restoring the ground to its former state. With the characteristic impudence of well-off tax avoiders, the residents, living outside the city, persistently lobbied for a road at the ratepayers' expense. They were as persistently refused until the boundaries changed. The path from the top of Pembroke Road follows the line of Baker's Road.

In the 1960s a major road building scheme, which included a huge roundabout at the top of the Blackboy, failed only on a technicality of exchange land. The Corporation wanted to compensate the public for loss of open space with a tract adjacent to the University Halls to which the public already enjoyed access. Even nowadays, the Council encourages and the Downs Committee sanctions unlawful car parking for the benefit of the Zoo.

Continue along the Downs keeping well clear of the traffic of Westbury Road (right) and Saville Road (left) until the White Tree roundabout is reached, and take Cote Road (becoming Cote House Lane), along the left edge of the grass.

This side of the Downs, from the site of the famous Ostrich Inn at the top of Stoke Hill to Sea Walls, has long had sporting connections. In 1725, men raced for a velvet saddle, value £5; maidens for a laced Holland smock. By 1749 the prizes were 3 guineas and a smock plus a guinea, but the value of the horse race prizes was £50. The games were so popular that another pub, the New Ostrich, opened in competition. Another sport was backsword, 5 guineas for the man who breaks most heads, saving his own. 'Vinegar', says the advertisement, 'by J.W.'. In 1778, there was a cockfight between the gentry of Somerset and Devon.

The heyday of the Ostrich was the fashionable period of Hotwells: breakfasts, dinners with turtle soup, and an excursionists' 2/- ordinary on Sundays. The landlord even sponsored lighting on the Downs.

Between 1828 and 1838 the race meeting depicted by Rolinda Sharples took place there. Thereafter, decline for the rowdier events, though the Gloucestershire club used the space for cricket. In 1863 the sportsmen assaulted someone who objected to their monopolising a public space. The magistrate supported the cricketers.

A white-painted tree will be seen by the roundabout **D**, which is the successor to the original 'White Tree', painted sometime in the middle of the nineteenth century to provide guidance to visitors to a local gentleman's mansion. Exactly which gentleman is disputed and at least three names have been put forward!

In 1950, two drunken Polish bank robbers, disguised in goggles and funny hats, tried to make their getaway on the No 28 bus from the White Tree. The comedy ended when they shot and killed a man in pursuit. Both hanged.

Ahead will be seen the imposing St Monica's Home of Rest, funded by the Wills family and built in 1925 by the Bristol architect, Sir George Oatley, who also built several university buildings including the Tower at the top of Park Street. To a fussing client, Oatley once said, 'Silence, sir. Give me time to think. This house will be here in five hundred years and for all you know you may be dead in three days, buried in a week and forgotten in a month.'

At the end of Cote House Lane, take path to right. At a footpath junction turn right and pass behind St Monica's. On reaching the end of Cote Lane over a stone stile, take path to left, dropping steeply. Down Brainsfield, across Reedley Road, along a path between the houses; left onto Stoke Lane, and first right into Stoke Grove, then right at the end into Red House Lane, to take the path through the extensive University sports grounds. On reaching Canford Cemetery, turn left (towards a Vodafone mobile phone mast) to reach and cross Sandyleaze. This path leads to Canford Lane and a few yards to the left a path carries on, shortly to drop left into the wooded valley of the river Trym.

At this point **E** we enter the extensive grounds of Blaise Castle, now owned by the City, but originally the estate of the Harford family.

Bear right to follow the river upstream, crossing to the other bank over the footbridge opposite when reaching a metalled driveway. The path soon enters the golf course keeping just below the tree line. Cross the fairway in front of you to a stile on the far side of the course. Go right and then almost immediately left along the river bank to reach the busy Falcondale Road. Cross over and take the path to the right of the BP Garage which goes through to Westbury High Street. Take College Road opposite bearing left at the Villager Restaurant into Trym Road. Turn right.

We have now reached the old part of Westbury-on-Trym which in early times was more important than Bristol, a small monastic settlement being in existence here by about the year 720. In College Road **F** will be seen the fifteenth century remains of a college, built by Bishop Carpenter, which housed a group of secular canons. The bishop styled himself 'Bishop of Worcester and Westbury' in an attempt to extend his influence to Bristol, by then becoming increasingly important. Two small towers have been incorporated into a block of old peoples flats. The gatehouse is owned by the National Trust and may be visited by prior arrangement.

Turn right into Chock Lane, and immediately right again onto a path between the cottages, and leading through the churchyard of Holy Trinity Church to Church Road and thence to the centre of Westbury village, where refreshments and buses will be found.

There are many old cottages to be seen in Trym Road and Chock Lane, and the church **G** (usually open) and dating from the thirteenth century is well worth a visit. The church was enlarged and improved by Bishop Carpenter as part of his campaign to increase his influence in the area. Immediately by the church gates, No 38 Church Road (Elsie Briggs House), dating from the fifteenth century, is the oldest house in Westbury.

WALK No 15

500m
1/4 mile

NORTH

BEDMINSTER AND SOUTHVILLE

Description: *Another view of areas that lay outside the traditional city boundary.*
Length: *5 miles.*
Refreshments: *Pubs and cafés en route.*
Transport: *Several buses serve Bedminster. There is no link between the beginning and end of the walk described.*

Bristol has been established since the eleventh century as a port, but Bedminster, just south of the river Avon and now part of Bristol, has been established even longer. Some believe it was Roman; certainly there was a Saxon settlement. However, most of the buildings that you see in Bedminster today relate to Bristol's Victorian industrial past and the working people in that community - tobacco warehouses and factories and coal mines, non-conformist churches and chapels, old-fashioned Victorian shops and pubs.

Bedminster is still a lively and friendly community, with a clear sense of its own identity separate from Bristol. The factories and coal-mines closed years ago and have now been converted into offices, an arts space and a children's playground, but the community itself still thrives.

By the middle ages, Bedminster was a thriving rural area - its rural past can be seen today in pub names such as the Barley Mow, the Spotted Cow and the Three Horseshoes - centred around St John's Church, which sadly no longer exists. The imposing fifteenth century church was destroyed in 1644 during the Civil War, and a rather modest replacement was built in 1663. By the middle of the 1800s, the population of Bedminster had increased enormously and St John's church was rebuilt in a far more imposing style in 1855. Sadly, this church was destroyed during a Luftwaffe raid on Good Friday 1941, and the ruins were eventually demolished in 1962. In its time, St John's church was the major church of Bedminster, and St Mary Redcliffe was merely a daughter church of St John's.

The walk starts at Bedminster Library **A**. *With your back to the entrance to the Library, walk straight ahead along East Street.*

The junction of East Street and Philip Street was a thriving hamlet within Bedminster called Brightbow. From this point, you can see the Barley Mow pub and one of Bedminster's many church halls behind. The Windmill Hill City Farm is close by. You can see the former factories and offices of the tobacco firm W.D. & H.O. Wills - now an attractively renovated shopping precinct - and the shops of East Street. Methodism was very strong in Bedminster, and Wesley preached on at least four occasions here in 'The Paddock', which is probably where ASDA's car park now is. Note the tall tower of the old police/fire station - this was a watchtower for fires.

Turn right into Lombard Street, and follow the road round the bend until you see the ASDA car park on your right. Immediately opposite the car entrance to ASDA is a cul-de-sac, but with pedestrian access. This is Southville Place. Turn left along Southville Place, then at the end turn right then immediately left along Southville Road.

Here you can see St Paul's church **B**. The Bishop of Bath and Wells, an opponent of Reform, was mobbed when he came to consecrate it in 1831. (At that date, Bedminster was in Somerset whilst the See of Bristol covered the City and Dorset.) There was also an ecclesiological dispute. The altar screen 'frightened one or two nervous people, who fear that every sign of good taste is a "mark of the beast" and that the Devil and the Pope are sure to be concealed in everything that is not incongruous in design and barbarously out of place'. St Paul's was gutted during the war. In recent years the building has been struck by lightning.

The church fronts on the busy Coronation Road, running alongside the New Cut on an embankment of spoil. It used to be a favourite course for running matches in which some of the Grace brothers competed. In 1873 Thomas Proctor spent £500 planting trees along the riverside. 'A foolish attempt [was] made to style this parade a boulevard but the public ... declined to adopt the misnomer.' Proctor's other benefactions included the

Mansion House and a service of civic plate. The drinking fountain on Clifton Down for which he left £100 in his will, was impiously moved to speed up traffic.

Directly opposite the front entrance of the church is a ramp leading down to the old Gaol Ferry (on the 1903 OS map, it appears as Coronation Ferry), replaced by a suspension bridge in 1935.

The New Gaol gatehouse, a place of public execution until the practice was abolished, still stands on the opposite bank. The first execution in 1821 drew a huge crowd. Unfortunately the executioner lost his nerve and hid himself as soon as he observed the near approach of the criminal. After some search he was found behind a door and brought upon the scaffold. Tactfully, at the gathering before the event, the BRI surgeon whose duty it was to anatomise the body was not introduced to the prisoner. He had himself given evidence at the trial, though it is at least arguable that the death was caused not directly by assault with a lump of rock but by unhygienic hospital treatment. The surgeon made a mistake with the paperwork so he had to come back later to collect the body in a coach. Eventually, he had the skin tanned as a book-binding.

One can only admire the style of Mrs Burdock, the poisoner, who, wearing an expensive dress, demanded an umbrella as she waited on the scaffold. (In another version of the story, she was offered an umbrella and said 'No need to bother now. I shan't be wearing this lot again'.)

Turn left down Acraman's Road This comes out to Alpha Road and the endearing (but sadly defunct) Bristol Dolls' Hospital. Turn left into Alpha Road then bear right into Dean Lane.

Acraman's Road was named after the man who owned the plot of land on which the church now stands. The story of Bedminster and Southville in the last 150 years is also the story of the Smyth family. They owned most of Bedminster, including Ashton Court, and the mark of the family is to be seen everywhere. Kingswood was already a mining area, and Sir Greville Smyth commissioned a mining survey to see if there were coal deposits in Bedminster too. There were, and the first pit was opened in South Liberty Lane in 1744. By 1830, eighteen pits were in operation, the biggest of which was in Dean Lane. This can still be seen in Dame Emily Park **C** (named after Greville Smyth's wife), to be seen shortly on your right, where a set of railings (and formerly a bandstand) mark the covered top of the area's biggest pit. The last pit closed in 1924.

Dean Lane comes out to the junction of North Street and Cannon Street, by a pub now called the Aurora **D** (until recently called The Star, then the Florikin and Firkin). This pub has a colourful history - in the 1830s, the landlord purchased a live tiger from Bristol Docks, which he displayed in a cage in the pub. This drew the crowds for a while, but the novelty wore off. So to boost crowds further, the landlord took to getting into the cage with the tiger. This ploy worked, and would probably have made the landlord rich, were it not for the inevitable night when the tiger killed and ate the unfortunate man!

Turn right along North Street.

Just past the Aurora by the zebra crossing, glance up at the corner house on Merrywood Road - 'Poets Corner 1882' **E**. Southey and Coleridge both had Bedminster connections, but this corner is not dedicated to them. A butcher's shop once stood here, owned by the brother of the butcher whose shop still stands further up North Street (Collard's). He was renowned for his awful music-hall style poetry, and the monument was erected as a joke.

Cross over the zebra crossing, turn left and round into Cannon Street (this involves doubling back a few metres, as the Merrywood Road 'Poets Corner' is actually a minor detour).

You can see the Robert Fitzharding pub on the left. The Fitzhardings were lords of the manor of Bedminster between the twelfth and sixteenth centuries. The Robert Fitzharding after whom this pub is named was a rich merchant who founded Bristol Cathedral.

Cannon Street also housed the Town Hall of Bedminster (where Clara Butt gave her first performance), and three haberdashery shops owned by E.N. Miles (where the advertising hoardings now are). Over to the left you can see Cameron Balloons **F**, and the Robinsons Paper Bag factory. The Cameron Balloons building was in fact the first Robinsons paper bag factory, built in the 1880s. By 1897, they had expanded and built a second big block. This is now unoccupied, but the company name can still be seen from behind the building.

Just past the Robert Fitzharding pub, turn right into British Road.

This was originally called Victoria Street, but was renamed British Road in 1846. The non-conformists competed against the 'National Schools', mainly founded by the Church of England, and set up their own 'British Schools', a major one being on this road and giving the later name to the road. The school had many uses after its closure, but had been standing empty for several years when it was vandalised in 1997. It was demolished a year later, and little remains apart from a single wall still standing. The Lam Rim Buddhist centre can be seen in Victoria Place - this is also a complementary health centre. The Princess of Wales is an early nineteenth century pub, and the pub sign with the picture of Princess Diana is recent - the sign formerly showed Alexandra, the wife of Edward VII.

Ebenezer Methodist church in British Road is a modern church, replacing the grand neo-classical church of 1837 which stood until 1980.

Turn right into Hebron Road. The bottom of Hebron Road comes out onto North Street. Make a minor detour here by turning right into North Street.

The magnificent Hebron Chapel **G**, was built as a chapel by a breakaway Methodist group and later became a Spiritualist church. The overgrown burial ground contains the grave of the exotically named Princess Caribou. In fact, the 'princess' was a poor Devonian woman named Mary Baker who pretended to be a Javanese princess and was fêted by the wealthy and famous in the early 1800s. She died a pauper in 1868.

A couple of houses down along North Street is A.D. Collard, the butcher (now closed). It still has the original tiles on the shop front and some original wrought iron fittings **H**. The Collards were originally a French Huguenot family and established themselves in Bedminster in the 1850s.

Double back along North Street in the other direction. At the Hen and Chicken, turn right into Greville Road.

You will see Gaywood House on your left. This is now a doctor's surgery and tower block, and replaced a graceful eighteenth century building called Dorset House. Further on is the Spotted Cow (another reference to Bedminster's rural past) and then the Hen and Chicken pub. This traditional Bedminster pub became nationally famous in the early 1990s when it became Bristol's first theatre pub **I**, and hosted the very talented Show of Strength theatre company. Most performances were sold out, and people came from all over the U.K. to see their performances, which received glowing reviews in national broadsheets such as the Guardian and Observer. The theatre group are still performing, and are not at the Hen and Chicken but instead perform at the nearby Tobacco Factory on North Street/Raleigh Road.

Greville road is named after Sir Greville Smyth. You will notice houses on the right with names such as 'Prospect Place'. These houses, built in the 1880s, used to have superb views over Clifton until the larger three storey houses were built later. Some of the larger houses have the house numbers engraved into the stone, for example number 173 on the left ■. However, the house with 173 engraved into it is not 173 Greville Road - it's 47 Greville Road. The reason for this can be seen by looking at any map - Greville Road has a 'dog-leg' in it. It was originally going to be an extension of Stackpool Road, and Stackpool Road now stops dead at a large brick wall. This marked the boundary of a vicarage, and the church refused to sell up to the developers. As a result, the brick wall stayed (and is still there), and Greville Road had to be diverted around the vicarage. The vicarage is no longer there, but Vicarage Road is.

At what seems to be the end of Greville Road, turn right (in fact, you're still in Greville Road), then follow the road round to the left, then at the top of the hill turn left again, and follow the road round to the right. You've negotiated the 'dog-leg' of Greville Road, and you are now in Stackpool Road. Walk along Stackpool Road and turn left down Beauley Road. Continue down Beauley Road, and near the bottom, turn left along Raleigh Road, then take the first right (it's quite a way) along Upton Road.

You can see the Southville Centre, a former school. This is now a thriving community centre and sheltered housing development.

The end of Raleigh Road was very industrial, and that part of the road was very hemmed in. The old tobacco factories were demolished a few years ago, but the ones in Upton Road have been renovated as offices.

When you reach the crossroads, turn left along Greenway Bush Lane. Keep going until you almost reach North Street, then turn right into Ashton Gate Road. At the end of Ashton Gate Road, turn left along a tiny road called Back Lane. This comes out into North Street near the old tollhouse ◪ *and faces Greville Smyth Park at Ashton Gate. At the end of Back Lane, turn right past the tollhouse, and then Greville Smyth Park. One path runs parallel to Frayne Road, but take the diagonal path leading into the play area of the park. Walk across the grass of the park and at the far corner you will see an underpass. Go through the underpass, follow the path round the corner and stick to the pavement - you don't need to cross any roads at this point. Follow the path round to the right under another underpass, and follow the path to a bus stop by a roundabout. From here, there are two possible routes to Ashton Court. The easiest is to turn right along Clanage Road, the A369, then turn left into Kennel Lodge Road. This leads past the University of the West of England and along a paved road to Ashton Court mansion. The alternative is to cross the A369 into the small road directly opposite, Parklands Road. Keep going until you near the end of this road, and you will see a narrow footpath to the left leading into Ashton Gate school playing fields. At the end of this path, you will see a stile diagonally to your right - though please walk around the edge of the playing fields rather than walking right across them. Go over the two stiles and walk right across the field until you see a kissing gate leading into Ashton Court.*

From this direction, you get an imposing view of Ashton Court mansion, the ancestral home of the Smyth family ◪, and the kissing gate leads right into the mansion garden. Ashton Court hosts major international events such as the Balloon Fiesta and a famous weekend music festival, and has dozens of different walks in its own right.

Walk onto the estate road and turn right past the mansion (if you've taken the pretty route - otherwise simply turn back and go back down the entrance road the way you came). This estate road leads past the University of the West of England and into Kennel Lodge Road. At the bottom of Kennel Lodge Road, turn left onto the busy Clanage Road. Cross the road and walk along the pavement until you come to a fairly concealed footpath on your right. Follow the footpath, which crosses a railway line. This path leads onto the Pill cyclepath and footway. Turn right on the path parallel with the river. Walk across the iron bridge.

This iron bridge **M** used to be a double-decker bridge, with a railway line underneath and a road on top. Before the Cumberland Basin complex was built in the 1960s, this was the main road from the South West into Bristol. After you've crossed the bridge, you can take a very short detour to the 'eco-house' almost immediately on your left, and the warehouse housing the CREATE centre **N** which is well worth a visit, with a permanent exhibition and a good, reasonably priced café.

After you've crossed the bridge, turn right along the cyclepath. Just before the cyclepath becomes narrower and follows the river, you'll see an exit on the left onto a very busy road (Cumberland Road). Go onto this road, and cross it with great care - there is a bit of a blind bend, and cars coming from your right may either bear right or whiz straight past you. Turn right along Cumberland Road, and take your first available left into a car park for the Harbourmaster's Office. At the Harbourmaster's Office you are on the dockside. On your right is the end of our journey, the Cottage - a popular dockside pub with spectacular views to Clifton and the suspension bridge - and formerly the harbourmaster's cottage.

Note: to return to Bedminster Library, retrace your steps to the cyclepath and follow it along the river until you get to the second footbridge. This footbridge will take you across the river and bring you out at St Paul's church near the start of our walk. Turn left and walk through the ASDA car park to Bedminster Library.

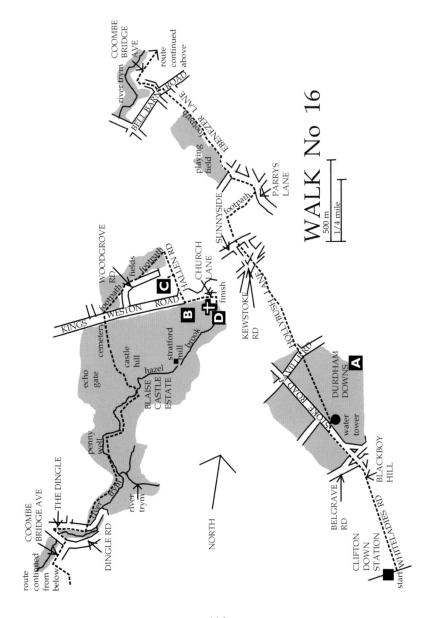

WALK No 16

500 m
1/4 mile

NORTH

116

BLAISE HAMLET AND HENBURY

Description: A walk through the open spaces and pleasant suburbs of north Bristol.

Length: 5 miles linear. May be shortened by about a mile by starting from the Water Tower on Durdham Down.

Refreshments: Many pubs and cafés around Whiteladies Gate. The Blaise Inn towards the end sells real cider.

Transport: No 1 bus links the start and finish. Many buses and a train serve Clifton Down. Except the 8/9, the buses all go to the top of the Blackboy near the water tower.

Start walk at Clifton Down station car park. Go up Whiteladies Road and Blackboy Hill to Durdham Down and the water tower. Pass close by the tower with it on your right and proceed across the Down facing in direction of one o'clock.

The group of pine trees on the right are called the Seven Sisters **A**. In fact, Bristol's best known group of trees became only three. These mature pines were planted to form a loose circle with one tree in the centre. This one failed to mature and one was the victim of the January gale of 1990. These have been replaced recently to form a new circle and recreate Bristol's famous Seven Sisters. The original clump was planted on a prehistoric barrow.

The University Halls of Residence are sited on the far side of the Downs, it is said because in the early 1920s, when Sir George Wills bought Goldney House in Clifton for a male Hall, the warden of the neighbouring female Hall, Clifton Hill House, threatened resignation. The University Council decided to build a safe, two wind-swept miles away.

Cross Saville Road and head down Hollybush Lane (sometimes a footpath), crossing two tarmac roads. Just before the end of this long lane take the footpath to the right (opposite Sunnyside Cottages). Keep to the footpath until it emerges onto Parry's Lane.

Two stories have been devised to make Parry's Lane more interesting. One is that the springs were used by Irish pig drivers so it is really Paddy's Lane. The other tells of a Parry who cut his throat by the well and walks.

Turn left and where this road bears left, cross over to enter Ebenezer Lane. At the far end cross Bell Barn Road, turn left and immediately right into Coombe Bridge Avenue. Follow road to the end to cross Dingle Road. Turn left for a short while then right into The Dingle, with the River Trym on your right.

Of the Dingle, an archetypal story was told. 'So beautiful was the Dingle that it had come to be regarded as a heritage, and few realised that it was private property till they awoke to find the trees cut down'. For once, things ended happily in public ownership.

Pass Grove Road on the left, ignore the first (unsigned) footpath on the left and take the next path to the left (where you see the sign 'Welcome to Blaise Estate'). Keep to the main track, later crossing to the other side of the stream and passing Penny Well on your left. Keep to the path alongside the stream and turn left over the wooden bridge. Go through the broken down wall, turn left and follow path up the stone and log steps (keeping the wall on your left). Continue on between Echo Gate and North Fort with Castle Hill to your right. At the top take the left fork across open grassland and proceed straight down towards the road in the distance, emerging opposite the Henbury Cemetery sign. Cross the B4057.

Blaise Castle House **B**, now a folk museum, was designed by William Paty and John Nash. The park was landscaped by Repton. Bristol Corporation bought the estate, 400 acres, in 1926 for £20,000: far-sighted munificence which is unthinkable nowadays.

The footpath is now to your left and runs behind Woodgrove Road - the path (overgrown at the time of writing) and stiles lead out to a tarmac drive. Go straight over and cross three fields to emerge onto a cul-de-sac. Turn right into Hallen Road. Follow the stone wall up on your right and you will find the entrance gate to Blaise Hamlet.

Blaise Castle Hamlet (National Trust)  is a totally picturesque estate village designed by John Nash and Humphrey Repton's son in 1810-12 for estate workers. Ten thatched cottages with tall pepper-pot chimneys, all of different design, cluster around a smooth green and the ornamental pump in the middle. In 1943, the hamlet was bought for £2,000 and sold on without profit to the National Trust.

St Blaise is not the patron saint of the parish church. A chapel dedicated to him was built on Henbury Hill in the thirteenth century, possibly on the site of an earlier chapel dedicated to St Werburgh. He is the patron saint of beacons and bonfires, perhaps the result of a pun on his name, as well as wool carding. He was also a healer of throat complaints; not because of lanoline and woolly scarves. He saved a boy from choking on a bone and was martyred with wool combs.

On exit from Blaise Hamlet turn right to end of Hallen Road and then left. Church Lane is on your right side and at the end of our walk, a visit to Henbury Church.

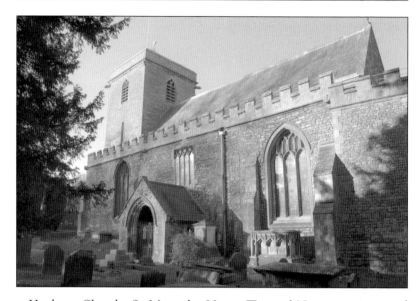

Henbury Church, St Mary the Virgin **D**, is of Norman origin, and Victorian restoration. The chancel is out of alignment, inclining north, possibly because, when the old church did not lie exactly east-west and in 1270, when it was lengthened, an attempt was made to compensate for this. In the churchyard is a grave that has long been an object of curiosity and pilgrimage.

Scipio Africanus, a black slave, was servant to the seventh Earl of Suffolk and Hindon who lived in the now demolished Great House near Henbury. The Earl, whose title on the stone is wrong, and his wife treated him like a son. He was just eighteen when he died in 1720. His memorial stone, decorated with black cherubs, reads:

I who was born a pagan and a slave

Now sweetly sleep a Christian in my grave.

What tho' my hue was dark, my Saviour's sight

Shall change this darkness into radiant Light.

Near the entrance to the church, on the left, is a gravestone depicting a crux ansata, or ankh, a cross with a loop as its upper arm, used in ancient Egypt as a symbol of life. This commemorates Amelia Edwards, novelist, travel writer, lecturer and Egyptologist, who lived at the Larches, Eastfield (the house was blitzed). For the purposes of literary research in male clubs and swimming baths, it is suggested she disguised herself as a man. Disliking Switzerland in its days as an English colony, she discovered the Dolomites, which she said many Britons mistook for a religious sect, like the Druses. The innkeepers there were astonished by her skill in making omelettes, not in those days a common British accomplishment. After a visit to Egypt, she started a new scholarly career. Her collection was large, including three mummified hands in the library and the heads of two ancient Egyptians in the wardrobe. Moved by the destruction of its antiquities she helped set up the Egyptian Exploration Fund. In her will, she endowed a Chair of Egyptology at University College, London, on condition that Flinders Petrie was appointed to it.

In 1827, morning service at Henbury was interrupted by a Government Messenger sent to offer Sir John Copley, Recorder of Bristol, the post of Lord Chancellor in Canning's Ministry. He was an interesting choice: Bostonian by birth, son of the painter John Singleton Copley, politically Tory, he had made his reputation by the defence of a Luddite rioter and a Cato Street conspirator. (In his new post, he appointed Sydney Smith as prebendary in Bristol.) As Lord Lyndhurst, he was known for the lucidity and legal acumen of his judgments. To succeed him as Recorder, the Corporation chose the atrocious bigot Wetherell. Of him, another parliamentarian said, 'he had no interval of lucidity, save the interval between his waistcoat and his breeches', which garment famously tended to fall down from the vehemence of his oratory. Famous for provoking the Bristol Reform Riot, Wetherell was also known at the end of his career for sleeping on the Bench.

For more information about Henbury see Walk no 19.

The bus stop is in Station Road, opposite the far end of Church Lane on the right hand side.

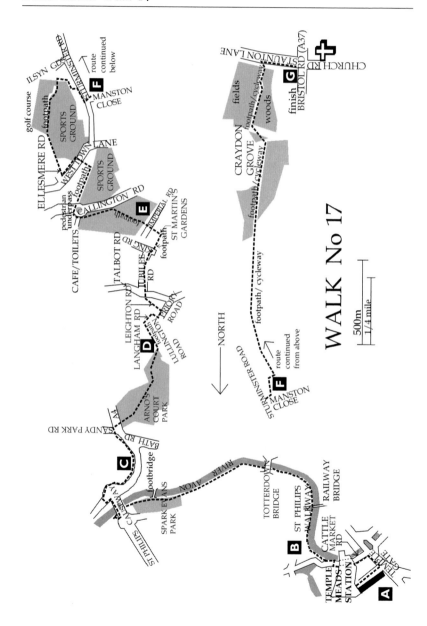

WALK No 17

500m
1/4 mile

NORTH

WHITCHURCH

Description: *This walk explores south Bristol, following the River Avon to*
Arno's Court, with high view points at Knowle, on to the
Imperial Ground, then along the route of the Bristol to
Radstock disused railway line to Whitchurch.
Length: *5 miles (8 kms). Time approx 2-2½ hours.*
Refreshments: *Café at Tesco, Callington Road, and public houses en route.*
Transport: *Bus return from Whitchurch to Temple Meads (55 and 376).*

Begin at Temple Meads station **A***, walking down the Station Approach.*

Pass The Old Station opened in 1840, designed by Isambard Kingdom Brunel for wide gauge railways and the earliest surviving major rail terminus in the world. It is now the home of the Empire and Commonwealth Museum. (See also Walk no 5.)

Left along Temple Gate and first left into Cattle Market Road. Continue under
Station Railway Bridge, cross road by keep-left island to join riverside walk, the
St Philip's Greenway (National Cycle Route no 3) **B***.*

The Cattle Market was held on the site of the Old Post Office Sorting Centre. When it was opened in 1830, one of the first lots was Mrs Gardner of Felton. Her husband accepted a bid of £5 10/-. This site was used as a burial ground during a cholera epidemic. Rumour was that not everyone buried had yet died.

Pass the disused Totterdown lock which is on the original route of the River Avon, before the Cut was built in 1810, linking into the Feeder Canal. The Feeder Canal gives access to small craft, but its real purpose was to keep the harbour topped up with water. The harbour was constructed to overcome the damage and inconvenience caused by the wide tidal range in the Avon. The story that it was the work of French prisoners of war is unsubstantiated. A contemporary newspaper reports the employment of English and Irish navvies on the scheme. At the ceremony of completion, they got drunk and fought each other until the Navy was asked to restore order.

Totterdown was the third lock entrance into the City Dock Floating Harbour, the others being at Cumberland and Bathurst Basins. Totterdown and Bathurst were closed in 1940 as it was feared bombing the locks would empty the water from the Floating Harbour.

Continue along the riverside, passing under a second railway bridge.

On the left is the Bristol Cats and Dogs Home, on the site since early in the twentieth century. The brick relief sculptures of various dogs on its riverside boundary wall was funded jointly by the Bristol Development Corporation and the Dogs Home.

Continue along river, under Totterdown Bridge and past the footbridge at Sparke Evans Park, then St Philip's Causeway Bridges. Turn left up footpath or ramp to the road then left to walk back over St Philip's Causeway Bridge. Go clockwise round roundabout keeping Sainsbury's and the Black Castle C on your left.

The Black Castle was originally built as stables, brewhouse, laundry and servants quarters for the Arno's Court Estate constructed by William Reeve in 1760. The unusual black stones were slag left over from the smelting process from Reeve's copper and brass works at Crews Hole. The castle also contains a chapel at first floor level which can be visited from inside the pub. Horace Walpole, the eighteenth century man of letters, or in John Latimer's opinion, a 'literary and archaeological fribble', called it 'The Devil's Cathedral'. Though Reeves was a Quaker, when a barrister made fun of him in court, he locked him in a room at the White Lion and said 'Here are two swords, here are two pistols; choose thy weapons, or fight me at fisty cuffs if thou hads't rather; but fight me thou shalt, or beg my pardon.' The barrister apologised publicly and lived to become Lord Chancellor when he invited Reeves to dinner.

Continue to the Bath Road, walking through the Arno's Court Gateway built in 1659 which stood in Castle Street until 1898 (noting the plaque). Cross Broomfield and Sandy Park Roads. Past the Old Bristol Tramways Depot, turn right and cross the Bath Road using the pedestrian crossing. In Arno's Court Park, take the tarmac footpath on the right of the play area, heading round the hill and up through the wood to viewpoint **D** *at the high point of Knowle. Here turn left along the rough tarmac service road. The view opens up from Purdown to Bath. Turn right up Langham Road left into Priory Road and left into Leighton Road. Pass The Knowle Hotel and cross Talbot Road into Jubilee Road opposite. Continue past the landmark Water Tower and the Baths, turn right into King Road, left through narrow footpath to St Martin's Gardens, turn left down stepped footpath crossing Imperial Road and continue on footpath down hill, diverting briefly to the open space viewpoint* **E**.

The view south is towards Knowle Golf Course and Stockwood with the Imperial Sports Ground in the foreground.

Continue on footpath and turn left at Callington Road following footway to the roundabout underpass (turn left if you wish to visit Tesco's café), turn right through underpass and right again to follow path passing school grounds on your left. Cross West Town Lane, turn left then right into Ellesmere Road. Take narrow footpath (between Nos 16 and 17) with stream on left and Sports Ground wall on right. At end of Sports Ground wall turn right then left to enter housing, keep to right hand footpaths until you reach Sturminster Road. Turn right then cross into Manston Close and join footpath/cycleway **F**.

This is the disused Bristol and North Somerset Railway line between Bristol and Pensford. It brought the coal from the Pensford Collieries which closed in 1959. It is now part of the National Cycle Route.

Follow footpath/cycleway to T-junction, turn left to Craydon Grove, cross open space following footpath/cycleway with woods on right and open fields on left. Continue to Staunton Lane, turn right to Whitchurch Village and the Maes Knoll pub (previously the Black Lion) **G**.

If you cross the Bristol Road (A37) you can visit Church Road and St Nicholas' Church. The previous church on the site was built in white stone, which gave Whitchurch its name.

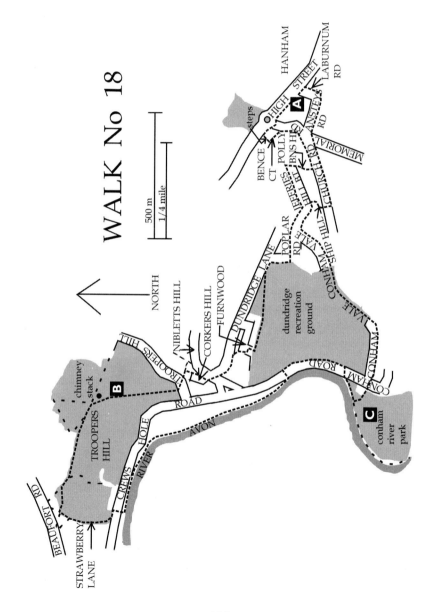

TROOPERS HILL AND CONHAM VALE

Description: *This pleasant and varied walk, with some hills, explores quiet back roads of St George and Troopers Hill, and includes extensive views from the top of Troopers Hill, the serenity of the River Avon Walkway, the Conham River Park, and the peace and tranquillity of Conham Vale.*

Length: *5 miles.*

Refreshments: *Maypole Tavern at the start.*

Transport: *No 45 bus from Bristol City Centre.*

The walk commences in Maypole Square, alongside the Maypole Tavern.

Maypole Square **A** - the original Maypole Inn was built in 1790. A large raised stone area outside the Inn was big enough to allow dancing. There was also a horse trough in the square. The Inn was renamed Crown and Horseshoe from 1901 to 1974, when it was once again renamed The Maypole Tavern. The actual maypole, currently within the square, was erected by the council in 1987. (Children have been known to dance around this maypole on May Day.)

Leaving the Square, walk down Hanham High Street towards Bristol. After passing the roundabout (Memorial Road) descend steps on left and follow the Strad Brook (original Bristol City Boundary Line) to the bottom. Go left, crossing the brook and up between the houses in Bence Court to emerge into Memorial Road. Go right and left 200 yards, right again into Church Road. Take the second turning on the right, and descend Polly Barnes Hill. At the bottom go left into Jeffries Hill Bottom, continuing on through narrow section. bearing left at the road junction.

Ignoring roads/lanes both left and right, continue to the very end and having passed the large detached garage on the left, ascend the lane straight ahead. At the top cross over Conham Vale Road, and continue ahead up steps at rear of houses. At the top, go right into Poplar Road. Continue straight on to junction with Dundridge Lane. Go left, and within 100 yards, left again, to enter Dundridge Recreation Ground. Keeping to the right hand line of trees, observe the vast open parkland, with its abundance of trees on the left. After passing the play park on the left, continue on to within 30 yards of the far end of the park, where adjacent to the dog litter bin, exit the park via the planked ditch on the right into a lane in front of some houses. Go left then right, to emerge into the car turning area in Furnwood.

Walk to the far left hand corner and take lane leading into Dundridge Lane (cul-de-sac). Proceed to Dundridge Lane and go left, down the hill into the narrowing road section. Continue on down to the next road intersection, crossing straight ahead (to the right of the telegraph pole) into Corkers Hill. Towards the bottom, the road narrows into a lane. At the next T-junction, go left to join Troopers Hill Road. Go right, across Troopers Hill Road (30 yards to right of chimney stack) and ascend the path onto Troopers Hill. Follow the obvious path (and steps) to the top of the hill, keeping the chimney stack on your right.

The eighteenth century chimney stack **B** was built to permit the escape of sulphurous fumes created by the copper works at the bottom of the hill. Sandstone quarrying was also carried out on the hill.

An Information Board giving considerable historical details about Troopers Hill is to be found as you exit the area onto the grassed area in front of Malvern Road.

100 yards beyond the stack, a seat has been provided should you wish to stop, take a well earned rest, and enjoy the extensive views of Bristol and the surrounding countryside.

Continue straight on and exit Troopers Hill in 100 yards via a gate/wooden chicane. Keeping to the obvious (left) path, continue straight on to where the path curves right. Leave path and go left through kissing gate, entering a track between bushes. Follow path to the end where at the T-junction, go right to the brow of the hill. Walk past two houses and one lane on the left, and take the next lane on the left (adjacent to a garage). Follow this leafy lane to the Y-junction, and take the left lane. At the next cross junction (adjacent to the lamppost) go left to the cross junction with Strawberry Lane, go left continuing to the bottom.

At Crews Hole Road go left for 30 yards, then right, crossing the road, and going through narrow alley, leading to the Avon River Walkway. Turn left and follow the river bank past modern riverside houses to junction with road. Cross over Crews Hole Road onto pavement and continue on for some 400 yards before re-crossing the road to rejoin the riverside path. follow path alongside the river for 100 yards and take path on left, up past steel handrails into Conham Vale Car Park (toilets available).

Conham River Park **C** is well worth a visit and is to be found through the trees on the right. The park has numerous paths, wooded areas, and picnic tables. Wildlife includes rabbits, butterflies, and numerous species of birds. The remnants of Conham Hall are still visible. (A pamphlet on Conham River Park may be obtained from South Gloucestershire Council Offices.)

Pious whale savers should know that Conham led the world in the production of artificial spermaceti. Dr Gibbes of Bath discovered a method of converting muscle into a similar substance, called Gibbesium in his honour. Lionel Lukin, a London entrepreneur, set up a manufactory at Conham whither horses and other such animals alive or dead that had become useless by age, disease or any other cause were brought. Their carrion flesh was refined into synthetic spermaceti for the better sort of candle.

Continuing on, crossing Crews Hole Road at the car park entrance, and walk up Conham Vale (signposted). The Strad Brook on the left meanders its way along the vale through a canopy of trees and the accompanying sounds of the many birds which inhabit these woods.

Follow this road/track (ignoring the steps on the right) to the end, where it exits (right) into Conham Vale Road. Continue up road and take lane on right, descending into Jeffries Hill Bottom once more. In 100 yards take the lane on right signposted Ship Hill and ascend the steep zigzag hill. At the top turn left and return to the Maypole Inn via Church Road, Ansteys Road, and Laburnum Road.

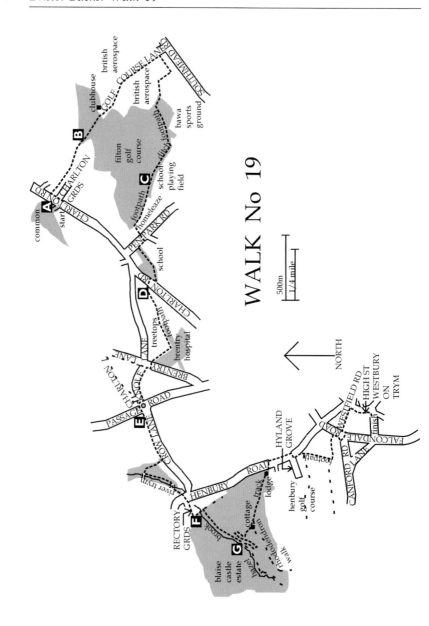

WALK No 19

500m
1/4 mile

NORTH

BRENTRY AND WESTBURY

Description: *This walk is a celebration of the open spaces that abound in northwest Bristol and provides an attractive, green route from Brentry to Westbury-on-Trym. The highlights include views of the Severn Bridges and the Welsh hills, walking alongside both tributaries of the Trym, a stretch in the lovely woods and parkland of the Blaise Castle Estate and a finish in one of Bristol's villages.*

Length: *5 miles*

Refreshments: *Pubs and cafés in Westbury. Salutation en route. Blaise Inn close to Henbury Church.*

Transport: *Bus number 55 to the start of the walk at Charlton Road, Southmead. Westbury-on-Trym is served by 1, 18, 20, 21, 22, 23 as well as the 55.*

Take the 55 bus to the end of the journey at the end of Charlton Road.

On your left is Charlton Common **A**, across which a pleasant walk is available using a permissive path. In the late eighteenth century, Charlton was notable for the agricultural improvements devised by George Winter. When he abandoned broadcast sowing in favour of a six-share drill plough, barley yield rose by over 50%. Yet more amazing technology, the development of the Brabazon, which was wrongly believed to need a very long runway, meant that most of Charlton was annexed by the Bristol Aircraft Company, forcing 30 families to move. The new Filton bypass was closed and replaced at Bristol's expense. The Brabazon never went into commercial production, but the facilities created for it were used for the environmentally indefensible, staggeringly expensive, stirringly beautiful Concorde. Ahead of you are the gates to British Aerospace.

Some 30 yards past Charlton Gardens, the last turning on your right, take the footpath on the right of Charlton Road, passing by a kissing-gate. The well-defined path runs through an area of trees and grassland before reaching a large well-cut field, used as a practice ground by Filton Golf Club. Climb the field diagonally left to the top where there is a signpost.

Catch your breath by turning round and admiring the extensive views **B**. The low hill on the left is Spaniorum Hill and in the distance can be seen the high ground on the far banks of the Severn.

Take the path through the gap and then, following the same direction, cross the fairway of the golf course diagonally to a group of trees before crossing a second fairway towards a gap to the right of the club house. A hedged lane leads to a stile which you cross. A putting green is on your left. Continue straight ahead down the road (Golf Course Lane). The road is initially tree-lined but then becomes industrial in character. By now we have crossed into South Gloucestershire, but loyal Bristolians will be comforted to know that we shall soon be back in the city and that Bristol has very much the best of the scenery on this walk.

Continue to follow Golf Course Lane to within 20 yards of the traffic lights at the junction with Southmead Road. A public footpath sign indicates a right hand turn. Follow the right hand fence of the car park and turn right with the fence by a low brick wall. Keep the building on your right and head for the right of the hedge ahead. (Don't worry, it soon gets better!)

Turn left into an enclosed path. There are playing fields on your left and more British Aerospace buildings on your right. Continue along the path for about 300 yards. The path swings to the right round the perimeter of a car park. About 100 yards from this point, turn left across rough ground to a public footpath signpost that indicates the route across another section of the golf course. The path heads slightly right to another footpath sign in the middle of the course, immediately to the right of the fourth tee. Continue in the same direction to a further signpost. We have now arrived at the county boundary and unfortunately the official line of the path is usually heavily overgrown. (On the map, it runs within the golf course close to the left hand boundary fence, emerging at a stile and path turning right to a public footpath sign at Homeleaze.) It is better to celebrate our re-entry to Bristol by turning right here and following the hedge for about 80 yards and then to turn left through the gap in the trees. Turn left and keep to the left of the raised green before heading for the left-hand hedge which is followed (in the direction of golfers' play) up to the crest of a rise and downhill to the left of a green.

Watch out for a surprise view of the Severn Bridge **C**.

The path then goes down a 2 foot step where you should turn left to a stile. Swing right from the stile and stay on this metalled path, keeping the hedge and ditch on your right. The Homeleaze housing development is on your left. The path later swings left to cross a grassy area before reaching a gate onto Pen Park Road. Cross this busy road, turn right for 20 yards and take a gate on your left into another open space. Head along the left-hand edge of the open ground to a gap in the trees ahead. Next, head diagonally right in the direction of a hospital chimney to a metal gate leading on to Charlton Road. Turn right for 75 yards before crossing the road and taking the signposted footpath. This delightfully secluded path descends to open ground where it swings left and becomes metalled.

Look out for further view of Spaniorum Hill and the Second Severn Crossing **D**.

At the fork continue left. The woods on your left are a little-known riot of bluebells in the spring. On passing Knole Cottage on your left go to the top of the grassy bank and follow this all the way along, keeping the woods on your left. Below to your right are the houses of the Treetops development. At the very end of this section, turn right and follow the path that heads downwards with the last of the houses on your right and the grounds of Brentry Hospital on your left. The path eventually becomes enclosed by trees and wire netting and becomes quite narrow. It finally turns left and comes out on Brentry Lane. If you're tall, mind your head on the public footpath sign! Turn right to reach Knole Lane.

A short spell of road walking is now inevitable. The most direct route is to turn left along Knole Lane and cross the main road by the pedestrian crossing opposite the Old Crow. A more pleasant alternative is to cross Knole Lane and to continue down Brentry Lane before taking the second turning left, Charlton Lane. Follow this for the whole of its length before taking a short path to the right of the doctor's surgery to reach the pedestrian crossing described above.

The Old Crow isn't the original inn which stood nearby from the sixteenth century till the road needed widening **E**.

From the Old Crow car park, continue along Crow Lane and pass the shops on your right-hand side. After crossing a side turning, Standfast Road, continue to a metal-gated path on your right, immediately after the bus stop. Across the road from this point is an important civic amenity - public conveniences! Follow the metalled path right from Crow Lane, keeping the playground and bowling green on your left. Continue across open ground to a small bridge. Do not cross it but instead turn left, keeping to the infant River Trym on your right. Eventually the path swings right to cross a bridge over the stream. Once over, turn immediately left to follow the opposite bank through trees. Eventually you reach the main road at Henbury Ford.

Note the handsome stone stile at the end of this path. Crow Lane was one of many paths leading to the pub. Over the years, the Harfords, banking Quakers who owned the Blaise Estate, closed and diverted them. With characteristic landowner's humbug, this was said to make it more commodious for the public. The parish suffered also from the enclosure of commons. Like the Old Crow, the Salutation has been rebuilt and remodelled to a Brewery Standard.

Carefully cross the road and follow Rectory Gardens, the no-through-road opposite. You will observe the Community Forest Path waymark on the lamppost at the entrance to this road. The road rises to reach the churchyard.

Henbury Church  has a handsome tower, and if you've time for a detour, a stroll to the right of the church will reveal the historic village hall and some attractive houses. Close House, (seventeenth century), was used as a dormitory for the Charity School endowed by Anthony Edmonds, a Bristol merchant. The foundation of the school was delayed because Edmonds's heirs produced a sealed document to substantiate their claim that he had revoked the bequest. The heirs are said to have put a pen in the hand of the corpse and made it sign. The school declined from a 'public' grammar school to an elementary charity school, adopting the Bell system in 1813. In 1815, the Severn flooded the lands which provided the endowment. The original 1624 schoolhouse was replaced with the present building in 1830, used for education until the expansion of Henbury.

Henbury was a favourite retreat for Regency merchants. The Churchgoer commented on its overpowering gentility, 'everything about the village being trained to look exclusive and aristocratic'. It enjoyed a genteel tourist trade. On Sundays, coach parties of sightseers were catered for by the innkeepers with a two o'clock ordinary.

Our route, however, keeps to the left of the church. Keep to the left hand side of the churchyard until you reach some metal railings. Go down the steps to an unusual tunnel. Walkers who are not as tall as the author will find this a more comfortable journey.

The right of way was interred in the 1830s because the vicar did not want one across his garden. The construction was well worth his trouble; the same family, the Ways, provided vicars of Henbury from 1830 to 1928. The fine garden is occasionally open to the public.

On returning to the open air, an enclosed path crosses a bridge over the Hazel Brook. Turn immediately right and follow this path through grassland, keeping the river on your right. After heavy rain, this section can be spectacularly muddy.

Eventually you will reach Stratford Mill **G**, currently being restored as part of the major project to improve the Blaise Castle Estate.

At the path junction, turn left on to a metalled track signposted Rhododendron Walk and start to climb. Follow the track round two big zigzags to pass a cottage and then to a further bend. To the right are masses of rhododendron bushes that provide a spectacular display in early summer. You will soon pass a thatched house on the right of our path. Sadly the house is covered with corrugated metal, following recent vandalism. (Note the signposted Rhododendron Walk on your right at this point for another day.) You continue along the main track until you reach the lodge gate at the edge of the estate.

Turn right into Henbury Road and pass the entrance to Henbury Golf Club. It is safer to walk on the left hand side of the road where there is continuous pavement. Pass the road on your right (Hyland Grove). Across the road and 100 yards further on, take the footpath on your right, keeping the wall on your right.

This is an enclosed path with the golf course on your right. Ignore two stiles on your right which lead onto the course. After the second stile, continue for 30 yards and turn left onto a path that keeps the other tributary of the River Trym on its right. On your left are the back gardens of houses. The path crosses the Trym and climbs steps to reach Falcondale Road opposite a filling station.

Cross this very busy road with great care. Immediately to the right of the petrol station is a path that leads you into Westfield Close. Follow the road to its junction with High Street and then turn right to pass the White Horse pub and the post office to reach the war memorial in the heart of Westbury. For those returning by bus, the stops are in full view from the war memorial roundabout.

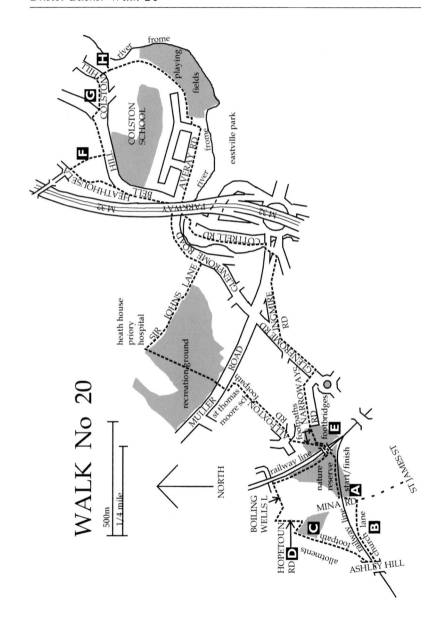

GAS-LAMPS AND CUT-THROATS

Description: *A circular walk from St Werburgh's to Stapleton and back,*
                    taking in some of the areas past and living history.
                    Complimented by Narroways Nature Reserve, Purdown
                    Panoramic views, with some gaslight thrown on the darker side
                    of St Werburgh's and Stapleton's murky past.

Length: *5 miles.*

Refreshments: *Pubs: The Farm, St Werburgh's; The Bell, Bell Hill;*
                    Merchants Arms, Stapleton Road; Miners' Arms, Mina Road.
                    Cafés: St Werburgh City Farm Café, Tesco Eastgate.

Transport: *Bus numbers 5 or 25 from Centre, alight St James Street and*
                    head for church. Montpelier railway station on Severn Beach
                    Line. Please do not park in front of the church.

Begin at St Werburgh's Church, cross Mina Road turn right and follow a
marked footpath, opposite church. Past allotments and rising to Ashley Hill with
the high railway embankment on your right.

St Werburgh's ◪ is now a climbing centre. Decommissioned for use as church in the 1980s, one proposed use was as a carpet warehouse. St Werburgh's church originally stood in Corn Street in the city centre until 1878 when it was demolished and the tower and some other sections were removed to the area now known as St Werburgh's. The reason for demolition was that it was blocking the increasingly busy thoroughfare of Corn Street where it stood on the corner with Small Street. It was already in a state of disrepair and was little used. There had been earlier attempts to demolish the church for these reasons. On one occasion none other than Colston saved it from demolition. St Werburgh herself was a Saxon saint and is buried in Chester cathedral. She was the daughter of the king of Mercia and a lot of the surrounding street names reflect her life and times.

If walking past the Miners' Arms on Mina Road en route to the church note the flood sign (one of several in St Werburgh's) commemorating one of the floods in the area in past centuries.

139

After several hundred yards you will come to a gas-lamp (still alight) **B**. Suggs and Co. of London made this in the early nineteenth century. The company still exists and is making the reproduction models as found in Clifton. Originally several lamps were in this lane; only one survives (one of 21 working gas-lamps in Bristol). The lane was known locally as Church Lane as it leads to the rectory in Ashley Hill, now known as the Ship Aground Pub. It was deemed unfit for a man of the cloth to live in too close proximity to his parishioners. Follow the path up across a small bridge; this spans Horfield Brook one of the local streams partly responsible for the floods. The tall embankment on the right covers the remains of what was once a local Manor House - Lower Ashley Manor, circa 1750-1824. There are very few details known about this but there is a fine drawing of it, showing a man fishing in the brook, in the City Museum (Braikenridge Collection).

When the path comes out on Ashley Hill, turn right, crossing the railway, then turn immediately right again following the clearly marked footpath down the opposite side of the railway. This will take you, through a large collection of allotments, to the City Farm. Turn right then left at Hopetoun Road, past the Farm Pub.

Originally the pub was the South Wales Railway Tavern although always known locally as The Farm **C**. There were always watercress beds here and it was a popular walk in Victorian days.

At the end of the short Hopetoun Road, turn sharp right down a track and into Boiling Wells Lane.

On your left is the oldest building in the area, Hooks Mills, circa 1668-1911 **D**. Boiling Wells is so called because a bubbling, not 'boiling-hot' spring emanates from the ground there.

Go past a very exotic house belonging to two local wood-workers. Just before the railway bridge turn right into Narroways Nature Reserve. Continue until you reach the summit, having crossed a disused railway bed. From here there are magnificent views of the city. Follow the path down to the kissing gate where the two railway lines merge. Turn left.

On the first of these footbridges **E** is the spot where a grisly murder took place on January 27th 1913. A Ted Palmer (a man of dubious morals and a heavy drinker) was so enraged when his fiancée, Ada James, broke off their engagement that he slit her throat. She managed to stumble down the lane to St Werburgh's church where, before she died, she managed to scribble Ted Palmer's name and cry 'My fiancé did it!' Ted Palmer was caught and hanged within two months. The lane became known as Cut-throat (other names included Goosey Gander Lane and Three Bridges Lane).

Cross over the second main-line railway bridge and go left up to the houses, pausing to look back on another panoramic view. There is a cut-through between the houses. Cross directly over to Allfoxton Road. At the end of the road a small lane leads around the perimeter of St Thomas Moore school. You will come to some concrete steps; go down these and cross with great care over Muller Road (named after Muller of orphanage fame). Directly opposite is another set of steps. Go up these and follow the path (this is sometimes overgrown and muddy); you come out on a clear hill, the beginning of Purdown. The former Heath House Clinic, a cottage, should be directly opposite. Once again take in views. Just before Heath House is a marked lane - Sir John's Lane. Follow this down; it will come out on Glenfrome Road. Turn left and follow road under the M32. Turn left up Bell Hill. Just past the bus stop there is a new housing development - Heath House Lane. Take the right-hand side pavement. Turn right onto the tarmac path as it leads away from the road. You then come to a junction of paths; opposite is a flight of steps. Turn right into the lane.

This is the second Cut-throat Lane of our walk **F**. This time the murder was in 1836. A Charles Bartlett killed his mother-in-law, Mary Lewes. The remaining dowry of his wife Sarah was to be paid on the death of Sarah's mother. It appears Charles Bartlett, a travelling actor, could not wait. He was caught, convicted and sentenced to death. The weapon on this occasion was a pistol. However I'm not fully certain this is the right lane - but never let truth get in the way of a good story!

Turn left at the end of this lane and cross over the main road to Stapleton church.

John Nelson, a renowned Bristol builder, built this church 🄶 in 1857. Outside the front gate there is one old gas-lamp holder, not working. However, follow round to Colston Hill to the right of the church. At the rear of the church there is a working gas-lamp but not an original. It has been restored by Suggs and Co., the original makers. This lamp is worked by light sensor so if you have a small person in your party send him up the lamppost to cover the lamp and it will ignite. There is a second working lamp in Fry's close (a private road to the right of the church).

Continue now down into Colston Hill; turn right into a marked footpath at the first bend. (A short detour to the bottom of Colston Hill and right up Wickham Hill brings you to Wickham Court, the Parliamentary HQ during the siege of Bristol.) Follow this track round (it can be muddy) till you see a set of steps doubling back downwards to the River Frome.

Go down twenty yards and you come to the ice-cave 🄷. This belonged to Stapleton Manor House (now Colston School) and was an effective early form of refrigeration.

Climb back up to the original path and continue down the slope until you are out of the woods. The path now runs between the playing fields and back gardens of Colston School. Eventually the path comes out at some garages at the rear of houses. Continue until the path goes to the left then sharp right. You will come out into a roadway. Turn left into Averay Road and continue towards the Merchants Arms and the M32.

On your left are some recently renovated prefabs. Behind some of them are what I believe to be World War Two Anderson shelters.

Cottrell Road, Rousham Road and roads named after Oxfordshire villages commemorate the Cottrell-Dormers of Rousham, connected by marriage with the Smyths.

At the junction, cross over the road which goes under the M32. Turn left, then right into Cottrell Road. Follow round to the bottom of Muller Road. Go over the crossing, walk on Muller Road pavement and turn left into Ingmire Road then left along Glenfrome Road onto the roundabout. Take the right turning up Narroways Road, a cul-de-sac. Follow the stepped footpath at the end up towards Narroways Hill again. Once again cross over two railway bridges, back down Cut-throat Lane to St Werburgh's Church.

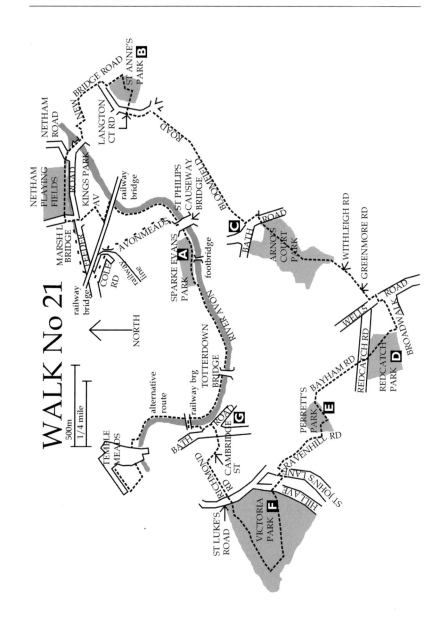

WALK No 21

NORTH

500m
1/4 mile

ST ANNE'S PARK **B**

NEW BRIDGE ROAD

LANGTON CT RD

NETHAM ROAD

BROOMFIELD ROAD

KINGS PARK

NETHAM PLAYING FIELDS

NETHAM ROAD

MARSH L BRIDGE

FEEDER

AV

railway bridge

ST PHILIPS CAUSEWAY BRIDGE

AVONMEADS

COLD RD

railway line

railway bridge

SPARKE EVANS PARK **A**

footbridge

RIVER AVON

TOTTERDOWN BRIDGE

BATH ROAD **C**

ARNOS COURT PARK

WITHLEIGH RD

GREENMORE RD

WELLS ROAD

BROADWALK

REDCATCH RD

REDCATCH PARK **D**

BAYHAM RD

PERRETT'S PARK **E**

RAVENHILL RD

ST JOHN'S LANE

HILL AVE

VICTORIA PARK **F**

RICHMOND RD

CAMBRIDGE ST

BATH ROAD **G**

alternative route

railway brg

TEMPLE MEADS

ST LUKE'S ROAD

144

SOUTH BRISTOL PARKS

Description: *This is more than a stroll in the park! And it's more than one park. In fact it's six. So give yourself plenty of time because this walk could take up to three hours to complete. It's a circular walk, all on a hard surface with one lengthy climb and one flight of steps.*

Length: *5½ miles.*

Refreshments: *Cafés and pubs en route.*

Transport: *Trains and buses to Temple Meads Railway Station. The number 1 bus links Arno's Vale and Temple Meads.*

The Walk starts from the front of Temple Meads station. At the bottom of the station approach, turn left and left again into Cattle Market Road to go under the railway bridge. Now cross the road opposite the pub on to the riverbank to proceed up stream along the St Philip's Greenway, under the Totterdown Road bridge and through Sparke Evans Park.

Sparke Evans Park **A** was developed about the time of World War I. Note the restored bandstand - a very popular amenity in parks during that age.

Still keeping to the riverside walkway, do not cross the pedestrian bridge, but follow the river to the far end of the park and beyond*. Eventually you will be forced to turn left away from the river, emerging into Feeder Road. Cross Marsh Lane Bridge, turn left into Netham Playing Fields following Feeder canalside path to rejoin Feeder Road at its junction with Netham Road. Turn left, cross river bridge and bear left to go up hill in Newbridge Road, taking the second right hand turning into Langton Court Road. Now go through park number two, St Anne's Park.

* Alternative route if the path by the river is impassable: after walking under St Philip's Causeway Bridge, turn left to follow stepped footway to St Philip's Causeway, then right and first right into Avonmeads. Continue past cinema following left hand footpath. Turn left under railway bridge and continue along Cole Road. Turn right into Feeder Road to rejoin route at Marsh Lane Bridge.

This would not always have been a pleasant walk. In the 1899 Bristol pantomime, the villain considered how to get rid of his enemy: 'If I could persuade him to bathe in the River Avon, that would do it: yet, no, that would be too horrible.'

At the end of the nineteenth century there was a long trial, involving nearly two hundred witnesses, when the landowner tried to suppress a ferry and close the paths to it. The St Anne's Ferry had been used for centuries. In the Middle Ages, it took pilgrims to the shrine at St Anne's Well. With the industrial development of east Bristol, it was a way to work, whilst St Anne's itself was still a beauty spot. Local opposition and the intervention of the Bristol and District Footpath Preservation Society saved the ferry and the paths leading to it. In 1957, the footbridge replaced the ferry. In 1923, the woods were sold to the city. St Anne's Park itself dates from 1900.

The Langton Court Hotel was built on the site of the original Langton Court Manor House, Brislington's second, which was almost completely demolished in 1902. The Lacy family of Shipton-under-Wychwood in Oxfordshire bought the manor of Brislington in 1586. Built between 1590 and 1610, the house was extended circa 1620 and again in 1667 when it was purchased by Sir Thomas Langton, a Bristol merchant, Alderman and, in 1666, Mayor. In 1663, he lent £50 to the Corporation towards the cost of a banquet for the King and Queen. In the same year, for purposes of tax evasion, his goods were valued at £9. (Colston himself declared £4.) His descendants became the Gore-Langtons in 1783, inheriting the title Earl Temple of Stowe in 1892. The oldest part of the house still survives in Highworth Road.

Over Langton Road railway bridge, turn right down Bloomfield Road to Arno's Court on Bath Road. You can now cross the main road to Arno's Park.

The gateway to Arno's Castle **C**, with the Black Castle behind, is connected to Arno's Court mansion by a tunnel under the road. The name is said to originate from a copy of one of the banks of the River Arno in Italy. The courtyard of the Black Castle (known locally as 'The Devil's Cathedral', a phrase coined by Horace Walpole) was built by William Reeve out of black slag from his copper smelter at Crews Hole. He built Arno's Court mansion about 1760 and the Black Castle was used as his stables. Arno's Court became a convent about 1851.

Opposite Arno's Court, the Brislington tram depot, built 1898, has an ornate clock tower. The last tram ran in September 1938.

*Follow the main path to top left corner and climb up Withleigh Road to Wells Road. At traffic lights, turn down Broad Walk and right into Redcatch Park **D**.*

Redcatch Park took its name from Redcatch Lane, now Redcatch Road, which was called after Catch House Farm, extending over 80 acres. On 19th March 1873 the Prince of Wales opened the Knowle race-course which ran across the southwest of the park. An estimated crowd of 100,000 were in attendance but the race-course's popularity was short-lived and it closed, a financial failure, in 1880. The pavilion was said to hold 8,000 people. The original Knowle golf course was laid out on the site of the old race-course but it was moved to Stockwood when the housing came in the 1930s. The park was laid out on allotments.

*On exit, proceed along Bayham Road and down through Perrett's Park **E**.*

Bounded by Bayham and Ravenhill roads and Sylvia Avenue, Perrett's Park, laid out in 1929, was named after Councillor C.R. Perrett who had contributed £500 of the £1,000 needed by Bristol Corporation to purchase the land in 1923. A marble drinking fountain with copper mugs on chains once stood in the top corner of the park near the site of a spring which issued as a stream down the valley in St John's Lane.

Turn right along Ravenhill Road, left into St John's Lane and over pedestrian crossing, going through Monmouth Street into Victoria Park.

Like so many parks at this time, Victoria Park **F** used to contain an ornate bandstand which has been replaced with swings and slides. The fields which were at the bottom of the park were built over in the 1920s and '30s. At its highest point, a large drinking fountain was erected, marking the then Queen's Golden Jubilee, but it is no longer there. Also gone is a large Crimean War cannon which was used for scrap metal in the 1939-45 War. This was originally sited in front of and to the left of the park-keeper's house which still remains. The 51 acre park was purchased from Sir Greville Smyth's trustees in 1889.

Victoria was one of three Bristol parks where open-air schools were set up in the 1920s for the benefit of children, especially consumptive children, too delicate to attend ordinary schools. (The others were Eastville and St George's.) The theory was that fresh air, food and a more relaxed curriculum would benefit children otherwise excluded from the educational system. The classes, each with an average of 25 children between seven and fourteen, were open throughout the year. Even during bad weather, though the only shelter was the bandstand, attendance was usually over 90%. One day in 1929 there were only 13 children at the class. In the night, a snow blizzard had brought the lowest temperature on record. The year before, written work had been cancelled because the ink was frozen into solid blocks. In 1938, the Education Committee turned down the teacher's request that the children be provided with wellingtons. Classes moved to an open-air school in a redundant smallpox hospital on Novers Hill in 1940.

Now make a circular clockwise tour to exit at lowest point.

The brick structure to the right is the water maze, marking the end of the conduit from Knowle which, until it was bombed, fed a fountain at St Mary Redcliffe. (The dry fountain head is on the churchyard wall on Redcliffe Hill. The model for the maze is one of the smaller roof bosses in the aisle left of the north door.)

Cross St Luke's Road next to railings and follow public footpath sign that indicates the climb of St Luke's Steps. Walk along Richmond Street and Cambridge Street to the junctions of Wells Road (A37) and Bath Road (A4) **G***. A detour round Bellevue Road is recommended.*

In Richmond Street, on the left, note the plaque to Irene Rose, quondam president of the Music Hall Ladies' Guild.

On the left hand side of Bellevue Road is a plaque to Clara Butt, the first musician to be made a dame. At the very start of her career, a Bristol University professor introduced her to the audience, saying it was her 'de-butt'. From Bellevue, the unusual view of Temple Meads displays not only the architecture but the complex railway system. Pylle Hill which you are standing on top of, was cut back steeply to make the railway. Traffic from Bath used to come over the hill to Bristol Bridge before the new road was built on the A4 line. (The Great West Road from London was alleged to be one of the worst in eighteenth century England.)

Back at the busy junction **G**, note the resplendent finger-sign, denoting the ways to Bath and Wells. Dismantled in 1970 to make way for a grandiose road scheme that was later to be abandoned, it was put into store in a local council depot for many years before being restored and resited in its present position.

Descend the steps by the traffic lights on the far side of Bath Road. They lead you onto the footbridge over the river.

The railway bridge was opened in 1892. It carries the Bristol Relief Line which allowed non-stop trains to avoid the bottleneck of Temple Meads Station.

Turn left to retrace your steps along part of St Philip's Greenway to Temple Meads.

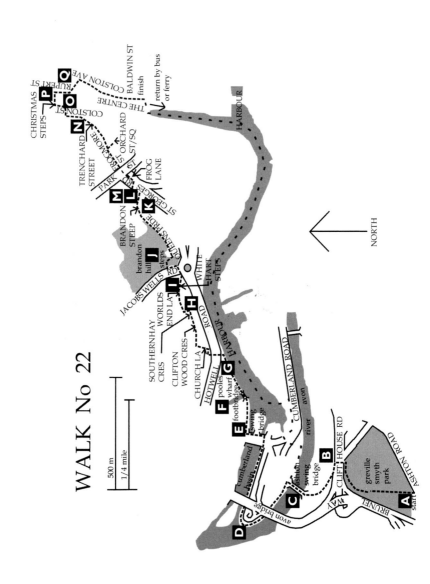

WALK No 22

500 m
1/4 mile

NORTH

CLIFF TOP AND HARBOUR

Description: *South Bristol, harbourside and some unexpected views from above Hotwells.*
Length: *5½ miles.*
Refreshments: *Pubs and café en route. One of England's best fish and chip shops stands at the foot of Christmas Steps.*
Transport: *Bus number 24 from Broad Quay to Ashton Gate.*

Enter Greville Smyth Park at entrance between Wedlock's Public House, dated 1900, and public lavatories of similar date, opposite the Ashton Road entrance to Bristol City Football Ground **A**.

Here on Ashton Road was one of the routes of the Bristol trams to the city centre. They existed from 9th August 1875 to 16th October 1941 when a German bomb severed the main power lines.

On February 16th 1907, centre-half Billy Wedlock became the second Bristol City player to win an England cap. Bedminster born, Wedlock with 391 appearances was in the First Division runners-up team of 1906-7 and the Cup Final of 1909: the first won by Manchester United.

Follow path straight ahead with glimpses of the Suspension Bridge through the trees. Fork right towards the end of the park and exit at the junction of Frayne Road with Clift House Road opposite the tobacco bond warehouse, now Bristol Self Storage.

Clift House was the dower house of the Smyth family of Ashton Court. Lady Smyth, the wife of Sir John Hugh Smyth Bt, lived in Clift House from 1802 to 1825. It was subsequently sold to Bristol Corporation and later demolished.

The imposing red-brick warehouse **B** is an early example of steel and reinforced concrete frame erected in 1919 by William Cowlin & Son. It is the last of the three built for the storage of imported tobacco in bond. Having been obsolete for many years, happily these buildings have each now been put to diverse use and are Grade II listed.

Cross the road and turn left, almost immediately joining the path on the right marked Ashton/Pill Cyclepath. Follow this path and shortly cross the River Avon on the Ashton Swing Bridge.

The bridge **C** was built in 1906 to carry railway lines linking the Portishead branch at Ashton Gate with the Great Western Railway line to the City Docks and Canon's Marsh. Until the 1960s it had a top deck which carried the main road and an attractive signal box, but its function as a hydraulically operated double-decked swing bridge ceased in 1936. Vauxhall Bridge, the next bridge upstream, is a miniature swing bridge, weighing 150 tons, as against 1,000. A footbridge, it was built in 1900 after the death of two passengers when the ferry boat was caught in the broken water of the Underfall.

On the far bank turn left keeping the river on your left and the second tobacco bond building, now the CREATE Centre and Bristol Records Office on your right.

The CREATE Centre would be more aptly called the Re-create Centre. It is run by the City Council's Environmental Health Department and promotes all aspects of recycling and resource saving.

Just past the CREATE Centre go through the iron posts on your left and keep on the river bank, passing under the Avon Bridge with its heavy traffic.

You will soon reach the commemorative stone recording that the construction of the Cumberland Basin Bridges Scheme commenced in 1963 **D**. Note the almost obscured slipway on the opposite side of the river where Rownham Ferry operated, and the excellent view of the Clifton Suspension Bridge downstream. Rownham Ferry was an important and lucrative crossing. Like St Anne's Ferry, it belonged to the Augustinian Priory that became the Cathedral. It is believed to have been used by the Abbot to reach his country home at Leigh. Despite the ownership, there were pious objections to the conduct of the ferry. The Bristol Churchgoer, who travelled by Rownham to St Paul's, Bedminster, and to Abbots Leigh, complained that not enough ferrymen, or as Leech elaborated, 'pimple-faced Charons', were employed to enable each to attend prayers at least once on a Sunday. Before the Reformation, 'if the boatman did not get mass, he sometimes got the Abbot's blessing *in transitu*; but there is little chance of a casual benediction now, as neither Dr Lamb nor any of his half-dozen Canons pass that way, or use the ferry, unless once in the seven years, when Sir John Smyth gives a dinner party'.

Rownham Mead was one of Bristol's tourist attractions, ranking between Blaise and Snuff Mills. The attractions ranged from water colour sketching to strawberries and cream. When the Clifton Suspension Bridge was built, ownership of the ferry had passed to the Ecclesiastical Commissioners. The Corporation bought them out for £10,000 in 1866. The ancient line of the ferry was across the main course of the river from Hotwells. It was moved a few hundred yards up stream on to the New Cut when the Cumberland Basin entrance locks were remodelled and some 'navigational obstructions', destroyed in the 1860s. These works did not enjoy unanimous approval. According to Latimer, 'a pleasant and innocent place of resort was destroyed by these operations, without much advantage to navigation, the rocky bank of the river below high-water mark being left practically undisturbed for nearly twenty years'.

You now join the roadway with Cumberland Basin on your left. Follow this, then cross the Ashton Swing Bridge at the junction of the Basin and the Floating Harbour, and go down the steps near The Pump House public house with the harbour now on your right.

A plaque on the east side of the bridge tells you that it was constructed in 1925 by William Cowlin & Sons Ltd, with steel from John Lysaght & Co. Both Cumberland Basin and the Floating Harbour owe their existence to the London civil engineer William Jessop. The Harbour was completed in 1809 with a number of adaptations to the lock systems designed by Brunel in the 1840s and further modifications in the 1860s. The attractive Italianate Pump House **E** was constructed in 1871 to house the hydraulic machinery and steam engines necessary to provide power for working the sluice gates. Previously the locks and sluice gates controlling the water level in the floating harbour were worked by hand. Hydraulic power cut the time it took to open a set of lock gates from fifteen minutes to a minute and a half.

Continue in this direction passing the attractive gardens of the new housing developments and using the turquoise footbridge over the dock **F**.

In this area, ships used to offload their cargoes of coal from South Wales, but in the 1970s Thomas Silvey Ltd took on the site and ran their sand dredging business. Their fleet of dredgers named after precious stones, including the Sand Sapphire and Sand Diamond, dredged sand from the sandbanks in the Bristol Channel round the Holms, sailing back up the river and, by means of a travelling crane, offloaded the sand onto the quay. It was gritty with a high silica content, eminently suitable as building sand, especially for concrete. In the 1990s, the business was barely viable as no ships bigger than 1,000 tons could negotiate the Avon with its tidal limitations and the notorious Horse Shoe Bend, so the company sold its sand business to ARC Marine in Avonmouth and the Hotwell Dock, now crossed by the recently constructed attractive footbridge, is empty of its romantically named ships.

At Pooles Wharf Centre and the Mardyke Ferry landing stage, turn left and cross the busy Hotwell Road by the pedestrian crossing.

The Mardyke Ferry **G** survived until 1967. It linked Cumberland Road to the Albion Dockyard. My father and many other boys living in Southville in the 1920s used it every day to get to the Cathedral School. He recalled the ferryman's hut on the quayside with its charcoal stove. Sometimes the boys would take over the oars, even occasionally losing hold of one, much to the frustration of the ferryman. The landing stage is still used as part of the 'water bus' ferry system in the harbour today.

Now ascend the winding steps opposite the Plume of Feathers pub dated 1799. At the top you join Church Road and soon turn right into Clifton Wood Crescent, shortly to become Southernhay Crescent.

Here is a little of early Victorian Bristol, undoubtedly more colourful now than it was then. Be sure to take in the view at the end of the Crescent **H** overlooking the harbour and way across the southern part of the city to Dundry Hill. The City Art Gallery owns a lithograph of a painting by William Muller which depicts this view as it was in 1835 before the terraces were built and the down was a meadow with grazing cattle. Today, across the far side of the harbour, the SS *Great Britain* is prominent in its permanent home as a Maritime Museum. It has recently been joined by the *Matthew*, a replica of the sailing ship used by John Cabot on his momentous adventure across the Atlantic to discover Newfoundland in 1497.

From the small square which you have now reached, fork slightly left and take the footpath down through World's End Lane where, if you are lucky, you will glimpse secret gardens through the doors which punctuate the old stone walls on either side. The path joins White Hart Steps.

The steps are railed on the left beside a cobbled path where donkey carts probably toiled up and down in former years. World's End Passage ∎ appears on a map of the 1820s, and in the poll directory of 1812 a John Coombs of World's End, Clifton, is named. The Bristol Street Directory of the origin of names suggests that the lane led nowhere in particular, hence its name. White Hart Steps were so called after an ancient public house which was demolished in 1877. The church of St Peter was erected on that site in 1882 and demolished in 1939. The present block of flats, St Peter's House, was built after the Second World War.

One is forced back to the twentieth century by the ugliness of the modern block of that building, where the path goes under the flats to reach the roundabout at the junction of Hotwell Road and Jacob's Wells Road. Cross this latter road and ascend the steps on to Brandon Hill. Note the old sign which includes the words 'No carpet beating before 6am or after 9pm' **J**.

Turn right at the top of the steps and follow this path which soon becomes Queens Parade, passing St George's C. of E. School on the left, then, when Brandon Steep is reached, note Brandon Cottage on the right which was the original 'Home of Bristol Savages 1907-1920' **K**.

The Bristol Savages was established as club for artists and art lovers in 1894. When leaving Brandon Cottage, they met in various other places in the city before moving to the Red Lodge in 1920. There they built the Wigwam at the side of the knot garden to display their paintings. Their strange name apparently stemmed from the fact that some of them were deaf and at an early meeting when there was a heated argument provoking raised voices, their chairman told them they were behaving 'like a lot of savages'.

You have now reached the junction with St George's Road and on your left is Brunel House **L**. This neo-classical building, originally the Royal Western Hotel, was opened in 1839 to accommodate travellers to and from America on Brunel's steamship *Great Western*, as the plaque on the building confirms.

Turn left and briefly turn left again at the end of Brunel House.

This is a diversion to take in the obscure courtyard garden. Here are the remains of the Horse Bazaar, where horses were bought and sold before the hotel was built. A fine bronze sculpture of a pedlar and his horse reminds us of the past **M**.

Returning to the road, cross it and turn left into Frog Lane (which shortly becomes Frogmore Street) with the back of the Council House on your immediate right. The Hatchet Inn (see Walk no 1) now faces you on its own traffic island. Keep it on your left and in order to see a little more of the splendour of Georgian Bristol divert briefly into Orchard Street and Square on your right. Return to Frogmore Street, pass Pipe Lane on the right and Lodge Street with its original cobbles of 1763 on the left.

Should you wish to climb the short but steep Lodge Street, you will reach the Red Lodge, built as a lodge to Sir John Young's Great House in 1585. Open to the public, it boasts a particularly beautiful Elizabethan interior and a reconstructed knot garden.

Returning to your original course, you are now in Trenchard Street.

This is a very ancient street. It appears on a seventeenth century map as Trencher Lane, but by 1770 it is Trenchard Lane. The Bristol historian, Max Barnes, tells us that here was the domain of Patrick O'Brien, a gentle giant of 8 feet 4 inches who was brought to Bristol from Ireland in the eighteenth century. 'One of his gimmicks was to light his pipe by raising the lids of street lamps. He was such an attraction and drew such big crowds that he only went out for exercise in the small hours - by special request of the police who were tired of controlling the crowds. When he died in 1806 he left money to ensure that his huge frame did not fall into the hands of body snatchers. His mammoth coffin, born by 14 pall-bearers, was lowered into solid rock and protected by iron bars. Years later, during structural alterations to Trenchard Street, his coffin was opened and a surgeon from the Bristol Infirmary examined the remains, recording that it was a case of acromegaly gigantism activated by the pituitary gland.'

Within a few yards you will notice an archway **N** on the left. Pass through this to come to another arch, this time gothic in style, together with a few derelict walls, all that remain of a Roman Catholic chapel founded in 1790. Within the ruins is a small garden and on one of the ancient walls a plaque informs you that the surrounding buildings span a period of 400 years. Restoration was carried out in the 1980s by the Bristol Churches Housing Association, providing 57 attractive flats.

Back in Trenchard Street you shortly reach the junction with Colston Street and immediately opposite on the other side is John Foster's splendid almshouse **O**.

We can do no better than quote from the history written by D. Tucker, Chaplain in 1988, who gleaned his information largely from an anonymous writer. 'Foster's Almshouses were founded between 1481 and 1484 by John Foster, a wealthy salt merchant who was Sheriff of Bristol in 1474, Mayor in 1481 and M.P. in 1489. His business interests often took him to the Continent and during these visits he observed the unfinished Cathedral of Cologne. In one of its chapels he saw a beautiful silver casket which contained the alleged bones of the Three Wise Men wrapped in silk. Foster, being overawed by the sight, later dedicated the Chapel with the almshouses to the Three Kings of Cologne (the Three Wise Men who visited the Holy Family at Bethlehem).

'At this period Bristol was part of the Worcester Diocese, so it was the Abbot of Tewkesbury who gave permission for the peculiar dedication of the Almshouse Chapel; the only place in Britain so dedicated. On the dissolution of the monasteries, the Chapel of the Three Kings of Cologne was spared although the Chaplain was dispossessed.

'In 1553 Dr. George Owen, Physician to Henry VIII, gave endowments of land at Redcliffe and Chew Magna to provide for 10 extra male residents, where previously there were dwellings only for 13. There have been modifications and alterations to the almshouses over the centuries and they were largely rebuilt between 1860 and 1880 when the west wall of the Chapel was rebuilt. The roof gutter supports are stone and each mason appears to have been responsible for a given portion of carving. The Trustees' initials are carved into the stonework.'

Turn left, having crossed the road to the Almshouses, and very shortly turn right to descend Christmas Steps, a rare example of Tudor Bristol with its quaint shops and cafés.

'On the left at the top of the Steps are some stone seats set in recesses; these are begging seats. When the Almshouses were originally built, one of the conditions for being a resident was that each resident put on a clean apron once a week and sat there and begged for a day. The little street was once the main road into the city from the north, so because of the attitude in those times towards charity and alms giving, a day's begging would produce quite a large amount.'

Originally a steep path on the north bank of the Frome, the steps were paid for by Jonathan Blackwell, a wealthy wine merchant, in 1669.

At the bottom of the steps divert briefly on the left into the St Bartholomew's Hospital complex **P**.

The Hospital was founded in 1240, the remaining ruins restored in 1984. The informative plaque is somewhat obscured by overgrown ivy. Here was the original establishment of Bristol Grammar School (1532-1767) and subsequently Queen Elizabeth Hospital School (1767-1847). The exchange of premises was 'a remarkable not to say scandalous transaction'. QEH had better buildings erected by public subscription on a healthier site. The Bristol Grammar headmaster, except for a token pupil, 'Lee's chick', taken without fee to justify his salary, ran it as a private enterprise. The next head was no better: a New College pluralist named Goodenough, he had to be threatened with legal action to get him out of the premises when he exploited a legal loophole to draw his salary without having any pupils at all. This cost £3,000. He claimed a pension. These are not the only scandals in the Grammar School's history. In the early days, the founder's family misappropriated the endowment, and a later head is alleged to have celebrated his arrival in the city by making a pass at a potboy.

When Queen Elizabeth I visited the school with her extravagantly feathered courtiers, she refused to hear eight verses recited by a boy masquerading as Obedient Goodwill. She had just endured twenty verses from Gratulacia.

Deeper into the complex another plaque gives you the geology of the site, it being the former course of the River Frome.

Return to the base of Christmas Steps and turn right to shortly reach the Centre. Cross to the left side on appropriate crossings and join Colston Avenue **Q** *which becomes Broad Quay after the junction with Baldwin Street on the left. The bus stop for no 24 is on the last bus stand. However, right opposite is the ferry landing stage and if the time suits why not take the ferry for £1 to enjoy the sights on either side of the harbour, alighting at The Cottage pub on the south side? Keeping the pub on your left walk to Cumberland Road, turn right and shortly cross the road to join the path beside the river. Soon Ashton Avenue Bridge is reached and the path on the far side takes you back to Greville Smyth Park.*

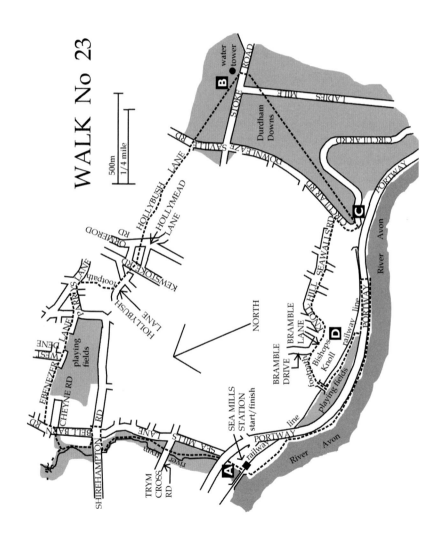

DURDHAM DOWN

Description: This walk starts from Sea Mills Railway Station, follows a
series of footpaths along the River Trym, climbs up to
Durdham Down along little used paths and returns along a
footpath by the River Avon. The walk can also start at The
Mill House public House in Shirehampton Road.

Length: 5-6 miles circular.

Refreshments: The Mill House. Ice cream vans.

Transport: Trains Monday-Saturday on the Severn Beach Branch. The
Mill House is just below Trymwood Parade on bus routes 41,
42 and 43.

*Leave Sea Mills Railway Station turn right and cross over the road towards the
small harbour at the mouth of the River Trym.*

A Roman ferry station known as Portus Abonae **A** was situated here
and has been considered the distribution centre for the lead and silver
mined in the Mendip Hills, though this theory has lost favour. The site of
the Roman harbour became one of the earliest wet docks in the country,
constructed by Joshua Franklyn of Bristol in 1712. The name Sea Mills
may derive from the cloth mills on the Trym which manufactured a rough
serge cloth. The Trym was navigable by ships up to Westbury-on-Trym
until 1099 when shifts in the land reduced it to a stream.

*Pass under the A4 Portway road bridge. Do not cross the footbridge over the river.
Cross over the Trym Cross Road, keeping to the right of the river, and walk up
the river basin to the far end. The path comes out opposite The Mill House in
Shirehampton Road. Take care crossing the busy Shirehampton Road and go
down the footpath running behind the pub car park or from round the back of
the pub in Bell Barn Road. Follow the path round to the right and turn right
where a small stream comes in from a small wooded gully on the right. If you*

cross the footbridge over the River Trym you have gone too far. The path leads up to Bell Barn Road again. Cross the road, walk left for a few paces past the unmade Cheyne Road and then turn right into a signed footpath between the houses, called Ebenezer Lane. This comes out on a sharp bend in Parry's Lane. Cross over Cross Elms Lane, then over Parry's Lane, at the bollards, turning left to follow Parry's Lane again. After 100-150 yards, where Parry's Lane bends round to the right and opposite Stoke Lane, turn right into a signed footpath which weaves right, then left, between the houses and gardens. Go down some steps and turn left at a footpath junction and follow this next footpath down a gentle slope. Keep straight ahead, ignoring left and right turns and pass by Sunnyside Cottages. Cross a road (Kewstoke Road) and go up the lane ahead called Hollybush Lane. Follow this all the way up to Saville Road on Durdham Down. Cross over the road and head towards the line of trees and water tower where there are toilets and a refreshment kiosk on the other side.

The drinking fountain **B** was erected in 1877 by the Bath and West Agricultural Society to commemorate the 1874 show. The water tower was built in 1954. 400 feet above sea level, it holds 600,000 gallons. The reservoir below, dating from 1848, holds another 720,000 gallons. Water was delivered by gravity from Barrow to Whiteladies Road and pumped up to the Downs. The company levied a supplementary rate on property more than 200 feet above Bristol Bridge.

Go across the road in front of the water tower and head half-right and cross Ladies Mile, a tree-lined road across The Downs, so named after the well-to-do ladies who used to ride along it but later frequented by 'ladies of the night'. Continue towards the far right end of the Downs which has fine views overlooking the Avon Gorge and as far as Wales on a clear day. This is known as Sea Walls **C**. *There is often an ice-cream van here. There are more toilets in the corner to the right.*

The drinking fountain to the right by the wall was erected and presented to the inhabitants of Bristol by William Hird in 1833. The house with a hexagonal tower, Towerhirst, should not be taken for Cook's Folly, which stood for centuries a little further along the cliff. The traditional story is that Cook imprisoned himself in it to escape death by snake bite. This stratagem failed when an adder was delivered in the firewood. In dull fact it was built as an ornament. John Wallis constructed a wall to stop people falling off the edge of the gorge. Unlike the prison-camp fencing now used, it did not spoil the view.

Let Cook and Norton tow'ring Follies raise
Thy wisdom, Wallis, will I sing and praise
Let heroes and Prime Ministers of State
Smile when they're called ironically, great;
Superior merit shall my muse employ,
Since better 'tis to save than to destroy.

Baker, the Sneyd Park property developer, claimed as his own a strip of land at Sea Walls which the public had always enjoyed. This, coupled with similar designs by one of the Worralls, caused such impotent indignation the Corporation set in train the process which protects the Downs for the citizens of Bristol.

Before Sneyd Park became too genteel, there was a pub at Cook's Folly. Because it had better beer than the one in the quarry hamlet on the site of Bridge Valley Road, one of the workers sent his nine year old daughter, Melinda, across the Downs with a jug. On the way back she was brutally murdered. The criminal was never caught.

Go to the right of the toilets and house and leave The Downs through the kissing gate in a gap in the wall on the left. Go along the lane ahead and into Seawalls Road and down Knoll Hill and finally Bramble Lane. Where this turns sharply right into Bramble Drive there is a Woodland Trust nature reserve named Bishops Knoll ◨, *the entrance to a house named Casa Mia and next to that, a footpath. The route is down the footpath but, if you feel adventurous and wish to make your own way through the nature reserve first and come out later on the footpath, carefully study the map in the entrance which clearly shows the way.*

Alternatively, go down the footpath and cross over the Severn Beach Line railway bridge. Turn left and follow the footpath between the railway embankment and playing fields until it comes out on the A4 Portway. Take extreme care crossing this busy road which carries heavy traffic from Bristol to Avonmouth. Turn left towards Bristol a short distance and go down onto a footpath running back alongside the River Avon. Keep on this path until it eventually turns right to arrive at Sea Mills Railway Station. If going on to The Mill House, follow the footpath to the left under the railway bridge and continue as indicated at the start.

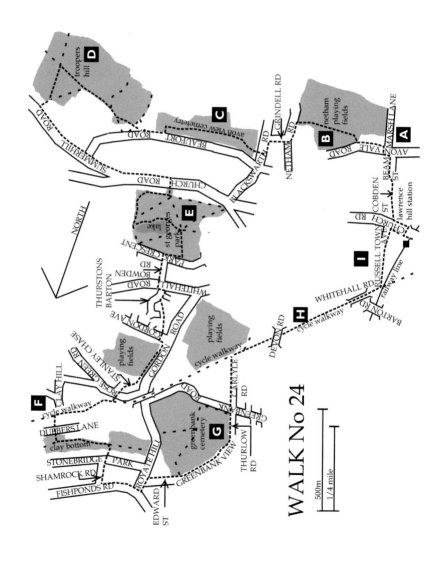

WALK No 24

500m
1/4 mile

ROYATE HILL

Description: *Two urban cemeteries (open on weekdays between 9.00am and 7.00pm from February to October, from 9.00am to 4.30pm for the rest of the year), an elegant park, ancient hedged paths, a hummocky hill and a panoramic view of South Bristol enhance this walk.*

Length: *6 miles circular route.*

Refreshments: *Public toilets, cafés, pubs in Lawrence Hill and St George's.*

Transport: *Bus nos. 6, 7, 36, 41, 42, 43, 44 or 45, or train to Lawrence Hill Station.*

Start Cobden Street (off Church Road). Walk up Cobden Street and continue to Avonvale Road ◪*. Turn left and cross road to climb up steps into Netham Recreation Ground.*

The area covered in this walk was industrialised in the early nineteenth century. The Feeder Canal, cut between 1803 and 1809, was built to supply the new Floating Harbour to overcome the problems caused by the wide tidal range in the River Avon. As a result of the Feeder, much industry was developed in the area. The Great Western Cotton Factory was opened in 1838 and employed about 1,500 workers, some coming from Lancashire. This was the factory which transformed Barton Hill from a rural country area where rich merchants had their quiet country seats surrounded by wheat fields and grasslands into a very industrialised area. St Anne's Board Mills, ICI works, Lysaghts and Feeder Road Power Station were among other local industries.

The tower blocks are the result of regeneration of the 1950s. The Council compulsorily purchased 722 houses near the old Cotton Factory and Barton House, the first tower block, was built in 1952. 'What Hitler missed, the planners finished off for him,' was a local saying quoted by David Stephenson. In fact it's surprising that the houses in several streets open directly onto the pavement even today. They had two bedrooms, a front room, back room and a kitchen. There was an outdoor lavatory but no bathroom. It is said that large families solved overcrowding by sitting on the stairs at meal times and sleeping four or six to a bed.

Mr Stephenson claims that one profession which never existed in Lawrence Hill is that of solicitor. I couldn't find a date for his or any of the other local history books so don't know when he made that statement.

This walk gives us an opportunity to witness the changing use of land. Under the vast expanse of grass are the remains of Netham Chemical Works **B**. 'Let me try to describe the Industrial side,' wrote E. Golding. 'Netham Lane was noted for the Alkali Works which produced sulphur, soda and sulphuric acid. These works were later known as the Imperial Chemical Works. There was also an engineering factory and the Cooperage which used to make thousands of barrels. Down by the Feeder Canal was William Butler's tar and resin manufacture'.

For many years, children played on the deserted slag dump until it was levelled and grassed over in the 1950s. But when and why were the great surrounding stone walls built? And why are the entrances from Rupert and Compton Street blocked?

Walk diagonally towards the football pitch and cluster of trees at the end of a row of houses. Take the track (known as a desire line by sociologists) and walk towards 'T' sign. Cross Netham Road, turn right into Grindell Road, then cross Blackswarth Road and into Avon View Cemetery through prefabs.

Tree lovers should be able to identify at least thirty different types of tree in Avon View Cemetery **C**. The tree-lined avenue parallel to Beaufort Road includes Fir, Silver Birch, Beech and Limes. The bird survey in November 1983 recorded sixteen different varieties including two migratory birds - the sparrow-hawk and green woodpecker. More recently skylarks have been seen.

Some of the local propertied families were buried here. Grindell, Herapath and Butler were important in local industry, and they and their families are here, some dying tragically young. Can you find a grave dated before 1881? The children's cemetery on the right was opened in 1995.

The grandest funeral at Avon View must have been Handel Cossham's. Thousands of people lined the route, and the procession of mourners took fifty minutes to pass. Cossham was the archetypal self-made man; the son of a Thornbury carpenter, he started as clerk in a Yate Colliery. He studied geology, formed a correct theory about the lie of the seams in the Bristol Field, and, exploiting this knowledge, worked his way up to own most of it, employing 1,500 men. Lord of the Manor of Kingswood, Mayor of Bath, and M.P. for East Bristol (he died suddenly in the House), Cossham politically was a 'Radical of Radicals'. He was also strongly religious, a lay preacher who left his fortune to found the hospital named after him. His life was the model for the hero of Mrs Craik's *John Halifax, Gentleman*.

One of the fascinations of urban walks is the constant change. In 1999 many of the headstones in this cemetery were falling backwards. The following year they had been propped up by sturdy staves. By 2001 the headstones had been secured and stood erect.

Walk up to the chapel and out through gates at end. Turn right into Strawberry Lane taking the path on the left until you reach a lamppost in front of a bungalow. Continue for a few steps then turn left beside a gatepost and along the path parallel to houses on left. Then go through gate onto open space with swings and slides in the corner and enter Troopers Hill Local Nature Reserve.

Walk towards the bench and luxuriate in the magic of Bristol. If you want to explore the extraordinary landscape of Troopers Hill **D** take the path on the left. You will pass cockspur thorn, hawthorn, broom and gorse. According to the display panel, woodpeckers, blackcaps, whitethroats and jays live here and there was a colony of grayling butterflies in 1885. 'A large steeply sloping woodland and scrub area to the south known as the Forest is a designated conservation area'.

The sandstone of Troopers Hill was quarried from mediaeval times until the early 1900s which explains the craggy dips. The impressive chimney was built in 1863 as a vent for the sulphurous smoke produced by William Butler's Tar Distillery at the bottom of the hill. Butler supplied the Great Western Railway. The fumes from tar were considered to have curative powers. Children with coughs were brought up the hill to breath the fumes. They also wore a tar rope round their neck during the winter. Added to the fumes from the distillery was the stink of tanneries, abattoirs and coal-fired industry from Crews Hole.

Leave Troopers Hill from the gate you entered and keep the hedge and three Lombardy poplars on your right. Take the path near the corner on your left and walk to Summerhill Road admiring the magnificent milestone stating 'Bristol 2 miles'. Turn left and keep on left-hand side to Northcote Road. Cross into St George's Park at crossing. Turn right and walk up the tree-lined avenue known as Church Walk.

St George's Park **E** is the most ambitiously laid out park in Bristol and its history is fascinating. Over 100 years ago the movers and shakers of St George decided to provide 'a public park or pleasure ground' for the inhabitants of the newly built houses. In those days St George was not part of Bristol and the project seems to have been run by their Amenities Committee. They bought up land formerly known as Fire Engine Farm and the Whitehall Colliery. Preparation for the park included grubbing out old hedgerows, flattening colliery buildings, evicting tenants, planting trees, erecting a bandstand, a urinal, a library and creating a lake.

The committee launched a competition for a design for the park. The winning design featured axial paths leading to a bandstand with an avenue of lime trees to Whitehall Gate. In 1895 the unemployed were being paid fourpence halfpenny an hour to prepare the area and the following year a caretaker was employed at twenty one shillings per week for a 12 hour day with alternate Sundays off (uniform included). But the hotchpotch of cheapest tenders and limited contracts caused endless problems.

Out of 450 trees planted in 1895, only 100 were alive in 1897 when St George's came under the control of Bristol Corporation. There was major disagreement about the cheapest method of laying the foundations for the lake compounded by the fact that the main sewer lay across the site! By the time the paths, the shelters, the ranger's hut, and a footway 10 feet wide to the bandstand mound 'using Cemetery stone for foundations' were complete, it was agreed that 'the bandstand was to be erected if anything left.' The magnificent avenue of planes (behind the library) were planted between 1901 and 1902.

Cross Park Crescent and walk up Bowden Road. Cross Whitehall Road at the traffic island.

Notice the plaque to the past on the brick wall on Park Crescent. George Whitefield and the Wesley brothers were conservative evangelical orators who preached to the workers of East Bristol from 1739 to 1788.

Walk past the prefabs with garages on left-hand side. Cross Gordon Avenue and walk along pavement which becomes a track to Stanley Crescent. Look downhill and cross to low brick wall. Join the Bristol to Bath Railway Path.

The Bristol and Bath Railway Path was constructed on the track bed of the former Midland Railway which was closed in 1976 but, thanks to the energy and imagination of campaigning cyclists, was converted into a route for cyclists and walkers between 1979 and 1986.

Turn right and take the second brick exit on left ▣. *Walk down steps, cross road and enter Dubbers Lane Allotments. Cross bridge and turn left. Walk with more allotments on the right-hand side until you reach a flight of steps on the right. Climb them, cross Stonebridge Park and walk to Fishponds Road. Turn left. Cross Royate Hill at traffic lights. Walk down hill and turn right into Edward Street. Walk up the steps on the left-hand side and enjoy the wilderness.*

Royate Hill Nature Reserve was saved from developers by local people and their supporters in the 1990s. Greenbank Cemetery ▣ was established as an overspill from Arno's Vale Cemetery in the nineteenth century.

On weekdays a tranquil walk through the avenue of sepulchres in Greenbank Cemetery is possible. If the gate is locked, walk around the cemetery. Cross Greenbank Road and walk up Carlyle Road and onto the cyclepath.

You can almost smell the nearby Elizabeth Shaw Chocolate factory. Sections of the cyclepath are refuges of wildlife, others are unwholesome. In October 2001 this section of the path was cleared of garbage and embellished by a small flower garden. Again, this attractive area was the result of community effort. In the spring of 2001, an energetic woman leafleted local residents suggesting an anti-litter day. 60 local people turned up, cleared the debris and six months on the path still looked fresh and clean.

Continue on the path. The attractive play equipment and the large building on the left are part of the Easton Community Centre ▣.

Before entering the building, study the outer walls. One side celebrates 'Under One Sky' which is Number 5a of the Time-Signs which enhance 32 buildings in Easton. The front wall has the following: THIS STONE WAS LAID BY THE PEOPLE OF EASTON 2ND OCTOBER 1989.

Inside there is a plaque placed in recognition of the work of Bristol City Council Direct Labour Organization, 28 September 1990. The centre was awarded the Gulbenkian Award for Community Buildings. The users, the workers and the art demonstrate the cosmopolitan nature of the area. The walls of the entrance hall were decorated by artists from Nicaragua while on a tour of this country in the 1990s. *Welcome to Easton* is a glossy publication which gives detailed information about services and facilities to newcomers to the area. The welcome message on the cover is printed in ten different languages.

Easton today is dramatically different from the industrial Easton of the past. This is how Ben Tillett described it: 'I was born in Easton, Bristol, on 11 September 1860 in a tiny house in John Street, not many yards from East Coal Pit. It was a drab, mean street and most of its inhabitants worked in the pit. The outlook was black, gaunt and smoky against the skyline. The buzz and musical clangour of the circular saw, swiftly cutting timber at pit props length, driven by an engine with a deep-voiced exhaust added to the industrial orchestra.'

Ben Tillett started work at the age of seven in Roche's brickyard on the Easton Road. He joined the navy at the age of 13 and before the age of thirty was organizing 'the so-called unskilled worker' on the London Docks. Strikes in London, Bristol and Liverpool helped to win the Dockers' Tanner in 1889. The magnificent mural on Stapleton Road Station shows a picture of Ben Tillett and his local doctor - W.G. Grace.

Return to path until you see the sign 'Russell Town Avenue' **❚❚**. *Walk down the pavement until you reach Church Road and the end of the walk.*

Much of this area was owned by the Russell family. Russell Town, Russell Town Avenue, the Earl Russell and the Russell Arms are reminders of the land-owning Liberal Prime Minister Lord John Russell and Earl Russell over one hundred years ago.

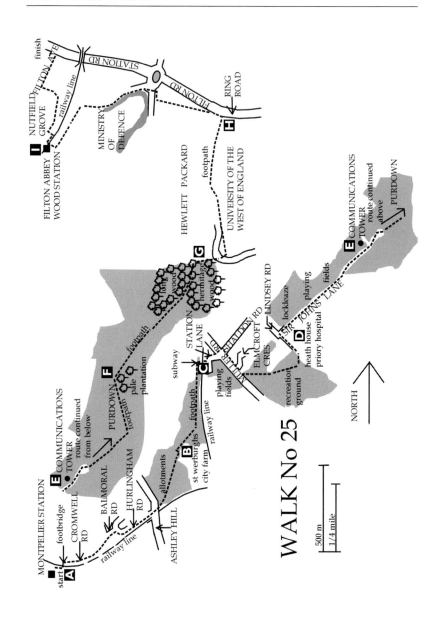

WALK No 25

500 m

1/4 mile

NORTH

MONTPELIER - PURDOWN

Description: *This walk commences in inner Bristol but soon leads along urban paths that beckon the rambler into open countryside with fine views of Bristol and distant countryside banishing the experiences of traffic jams and fumes.*

Length: *6 miles.*

Refreshments: *St Werburgh City Farm Café: Wed.-Sun. 10.00am-4.00pm. The Farm, King George VI Inn, Filton Avenue.*

Transport: *Bus Services 70 and 73 serve both the beginning and end of the walk. Alight at 'the Arches' (the Gloucester Road/ Cheltenham Road junction) and walk up Station Road to Montpelier Station (approx 300 yards). Return from the King George VI inn. Unfortunately, there is no direct rail connection between Montpelier and Filton Abbey Wood and neither station has trains on Sundays.*

Taking the footbridge over the railway line at Montpelier station, climb the steps to Cromwell Road and turn right. Where the road bears left continue straight ahead into Balmoral Road and then take the right fork into Hurlingham Road, which gives fine views of the city.

Montpelier Station **A** was once so well used by commercial travellers that extra porters were needed on a Monday morning to handle their samples. Even in the '50s, it was staffed by two booking clerks, four porters, a checker and a weighbridge attendant. Like all the stations on the line, it has since been vandalised officially and unofficially. The only remaining building has been brightly decorated in twenty-first century neo-folk style. The spelling of Montpelier was decided by the railway company.

The Lord Protector really did have a connection with Cromwell Road, but the farmhouse he used during a siege of Bristol was demolished by the Victorians.

On reaching Ashley Hill cross to the tarmac footpath opposite via the traffic island taking care across this major thoroughfare. Initially downhill, houses are left behind as one passes allotments on both sides of the path.

The communications tower, such a prominent feature later in the walk, can be viewed in the distance.

Ignoring side paths, continue straight ahead at St Werburgh City Farm **B**. *On reaching a white painted house turn left and immediately right continuing in the same direction as before.*

The railway line on the right is the main line to Cardiff built to serve the New Passage ferry crossing at Aust, then slightly diverted through the Severn Tunnel. It goes also, via Bristol Parkway, to Birmingham, the original Midland Railway link into Bristol having been closed and converted to a route for pedestrians and cyclists.

At a crossing path where the track ahead becomes a dirt path, turn right passing through the subway **C** *under the railway, which leads into Station Lane. On reaching the road junction cross both Muller Road and Shaldon Road at the traffic lights thereby turning right passing Elmcroft Crescent.*

On passing the final house turn half left to cross the field/recreation ground diagonally upwards towards the top (east) corner. Close to the corner there is a wide gap in the right-hand hedge. Pass through to the next field and very soon turn left at a similar gap on the left. Head towards an old stone gatepost at the edge of the field ahead noting the fine views behind of the former Brunel Technical College building and Horfield.

At the post note the fine views south and east over the city to the countryside north of Bath.

Turn left again across the grass with the hedge on the left aiming for another post opposite a house. Turn left into a wide track that borders Heath House Priory Hospital **D**.

Where the track meets the tarmac road, pass through two metal swing gates to turn right (Sir John's Lane). Continue the full length of the lane with Lockleaze playing fields on the left and views to the west. Pass the communications tower **E** *previously referred to and continue on to the dirt track. At the metal barriers continue ahead through the gap. Shortly veer to the right at a junction of paths passing through the gun emplacements of the former Purdown Camp.*

Continue on to a grass track in a north-easterly direction where a wire fence will appear on the right. Just before a gap in the hedge ahead, turn half left on an initially indistinct path and aim for the left-hand edge of the woods ahead, beyond which may be seen a burnt tree stump, partly black and partly white. Pass this stump **F** *but then turn half right along the edge of the hill. Note a gap between*

blocks of woodland ahead, not to be confused with a clear gap that comes into view after a short distance. On reaching a crossing track continue ahead veering left across the grass towards what now turns out to be a bay in the woodland boundary. A number of swing gates come into view; head for the gate at the end of the field beside a track gateway into the woods. Take this wide track into a wood that in season is filled with bluebells. Continue until a tarmac drive **G** is reached and turn right past the entrance to Hewlett Packard to the end of the road barrier. Turn left taking the left-hand path with green iron fence on the right, passing the University of the West of England. Continue on the dirt path ahead until the ring road **H** is reached.

Turn left down the ring road a short distance to the combined cycle/footpath leading to the M.O.D. Abbey Wood building. (An alternative, noisy, short cut to the King George VI inn is alongside the ring road.) When the cycle/footpath reaches a roundabout, cross to the white perimeter fence and turn right following the fence on the left to the 'deliveries' security entrance (not the main security gate just beyond the roundabout). Crossing in front of this security gate take the combined cycle/footpath to the entrance to Filton Abbey Wood rail station **I**.

For buses and the King George VI inn, use the station footbridge to cross to the opposite platform and take the path leading to the station car park. A path, left, leads into Nutfield Grove which in turn leads to Filton Avenue. The inn and bus stops are located right.

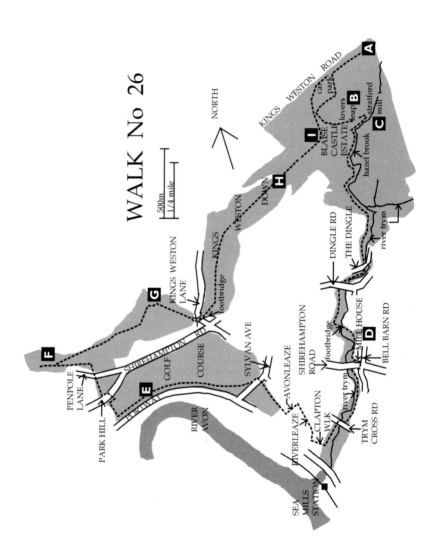

WALK No 26

NORTH

500m
1/4 mile

PENPOLE

Description: *This circular 7 to 8 mile, 3 to 4 hour circular walk can start*
either from Blaise Castle Estate on bus routes 43 and 57 or
from The Mill House public house in Shirehampton Road
below Trymwood Parade on bus routes 41, 42 and 43. The
walk follows a series of footpaths along the River Trym and
through the delightful Penpole Wood, Kings Weston Down and
Blaise Castle Estate with superb views over Bristol and
Shirehampton. For convenience, the walk is presumed to start
at Blaise Castle House.

Length: *7-8 miles.*

Refreshments: *There are toilets and a refreshment kiosk at Blaise Castle.*
Kings Weston House now has a café. The Millhouse. Blaise
Inn.

Transport   *Buses 1 and 43.*

Blaise Castle House **A** was designed by William Paty for John Harford
in the 1790s and Humphrey Repton was commissioned to landscape the
park. The estate is named after St Blaise, a Bishop of Sebaste in Armenia
and patron saint of wool-combers who was persecuted for his Christian
beliefs. A thirteenth century chapel which stood on the site now occupied
by the castle was dedicated to him. In its turn the chapel was built over
what was possibly a Roman temple. The present castle **B** was erected by
Thomas Farr in 1766 and originally had lavishly furnished rooms. This
strategic hilltop has a long history of settlement by man, being formerly an
Iron Age hill fort covering some 7 acres although the banks and ditches
are now obscured by trees. Later it was occupied by the Romans. The
castle is intended to be open from April to September on Sundays from
2.00-4.00pm. It is manned by the Friends of Blaise Castle. The house is
now a museum of household life in times past and is open from April to
October, Sat.-Wed., 10.00am-5.00pm. The estate is now owned by Bristol
City Council.

Walk up from the house past the toilets, children's playground and the refreshments kiosk to the car park. Turn left towards the wooded hill, noting the few wooden sculptures near the wood edge. Turn right past the sculptures and follow the path which runs inside the edge of the woods. The path bends round to the left where it meets another path crossing right to left. Turn to the left, where three paths lead off. Take the middle one leading upwards and to the right up to the castle. The other two paths follow the ditches between the ramparts of the hill fort and lead round the hill.

With the castle door behind you, walk half-right towards to a gap in the trees which open up to give a fine panoramic view over the river valley, known as Lovers' Leap. Turn left and follow the main route downhill, ignoring subsequent paths off to the left. Turn right on meeting a tarmac path. At the bottom you pass by Stratford Mill, beside the Hazel Brook, a tributary of the River Trym. Above Blaise Castle Estate the brook is renamed the Henbury Trym.

Stratford Mill **C** was an eighteenth century corn mill rescued from the hamlet of Moreton, near West Harptree, when Chew Valley reservoir was created, and re-erected beside Hazel Brook. Unfortunately, the stream is not capable of turning the wheel.

*Cross over the brook and turn right keeping to the main tarmac path. Follow the brook down the valley, ignoring the footbridges and crossing points over the brook. The tarmac path soon rises gently and bends to the left but still follows the brook in the valley below. Continue on the tarmac path as it turns down towards the brook again and crosses it, leading past a few seats. The path then curves to the right and rises gently while the Hazel Brook turns to the left to join the River Trym some distance way. Follow the path alongside a low stone wall which curves round to the right. After the end of the wall, the path opens out to become a small car park with the River Trym now flowing to the left. Continue on through the car park, cross over The Dingle minor road and pick up the path again in the woods opposite. This path shortly passes under Dingle Road and continues along a broad grassy area until it crosses a footbridge over the Trym and comes out behind the car park of The Mill House **D** public house and ends up in Bell Barn Road. Turn right.*

Take care crossing the busy Shirehampton Road and go down the footpath by the side of the bridge over the River Trym indicated by the Trymwood Notice Board. Continue alongside the river as far as the Trym Cross Road, cross over the Trym bridge and walk towards the corner of the field near the A4 Portway. Go through the bushes up the waymarked footpath leading into Clapton Walk. Turn right at the top and follow Riverleaze round to the left and up to St Edyth's church.

St Edyth's, 1931, was designed by George Oatley. In one detail, it was never completed. The gargoyles on the tower are still plain blocks of stone.

Turn left down Avonleaze and then right into the waymarked footpath at the bottom which leads on to Sylvan Way. Cross over this busy road with care. Go through the kissing gate into Shirehampton Golf Course, following the waymark to the left. Keep to the perimeter fence of the golf course which runs alongside and above the A4 Portway Road. Take care not to disturb golfers on the way.

Pause to enjoy the stunning views of Horseshoe Bend **E** in the River Avon and beyond. Horseshoe Bend was famous as a navigational hazard, a major cause of the City Dock's decline.

Continue down to the bottom end of the golf course and then take the path up to the right alongside a stone wall until it comes out by the clubhouse car park. Leave the golf course and cross over Shirehampton Road/Park Hill and go up the steps into Shirehampton Cricket Club field. Keep to the left-hand fence and cross Penpole Lane at the far end. Turn left and walk past the sign for Portway Community School Drop Off Point. Continue along the path on the ridge up to a small memorial stone with a seat running round it. Carry on a little further to Penpole Point where the path begins to descend steeply.

Penpole Point **F** is where the eighteenth century merchants of Bristol used to watch for the arrival of their ships. When the new turnpike road made the journey easy, excursions to Penpole Hill became fashionable. A Breakfast Room was built and its customers were permitted to ramble in

the shrubberies of Kings Weston House. A few fragments of the structure remain. Nowadays, the famous view has suffered from development and is largely obscured by trees. In Napoleonic times a beacon was placed here to be lit in case of invasion.

Return along the same path and just before the School Drop Off Point, turn half left into the woods. There is a choice of three paths at this point, so take care to choose the right hand path which will shortly follow the edge of another cricket field. Continue along this path through attractive woodland until you come to a clearing where two paths converge by two large boulders to your left. Follow the first path, past the boulders and go along the path leading down to the recently restored Kingsweston House. Teas are served in the house.

Kingsweston House **G** was designed for Sir Edward Southwell by Sir John Vanbrugh and dates back to 1720, replacing an earlier Tudor house. Mention of Kings Weston Estate and the Blaise folly can be found in Jane Austen's *Northanger Abbey*. The house became a hospital in World War I.

Requisitioned in World War II, the empty house was purchased by Bristol Corporation in 1948 and became a school. A college of architecture and sociology, and then a police training centre followed. The house is now privately occupied and used for functions.

Pass round to the right of the house and go up the drive leading to the gazebo at the top. This would have been covered with stucco. Note the amusing faces on the stone vases. Walk round the gazebo, go down some steps and across the iron bridge over Kings Weston Road. Follow the footpath past the large house and by the bollards into Kings Weston Down Nature Reserve.

Note the single ditch and rampart formerly part of an Iron Age camp at the far end ▣.

Leave Kings Weston Down by the kissing gate in the left hand hedge and go down a series of steps. Bear right near the bottom and then left into the clearing to Echo Gate ▉.

If the walk started at Blaise Castle House, pass to the left of Castle Hill ahead and walk down towards the car park near the road and then on to the house. If, however, the walk started at The Mill House, continue past the signpost pointing to Blaise Castle at the other side of Echo Gate clearing. Then take the footpath up to Castle Hill as described at the beginning.

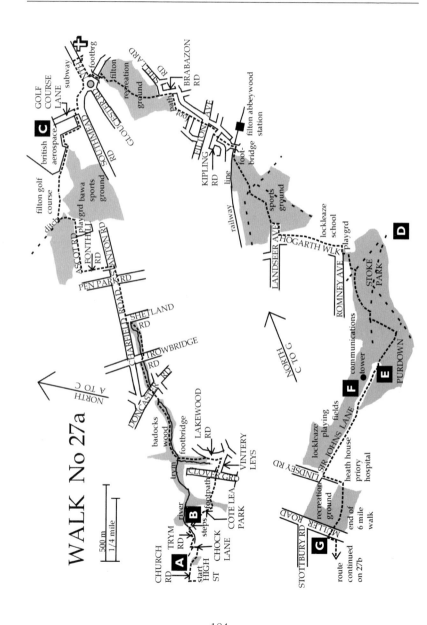

WALK No 27a

500 m
1/4 mile

WESTBURY - PURDOWN

Description   *This is a circular walk following a series of footpaths through delightful woods, parklands and alleyways with some short road links and culminates in a splendid walk across Purdown where the views over Bristol are among the best in the city. The complete walk returns to Westbury-on-Trym via more parks, alleyways and city streets. Public toilets and refreshments are pointed out on the way.*

Length: *6, 7 or 11 miles.*

Refreshments: *The (old-world) Farm public house is a short distance further on in St Werburgh's and should be reached in time for lunch. There is a café in Westbury Hill which closes at 5.00pm on weekdays.*

Transport: *The start is easily reached via bus routes 1, 18, 20, 21, 22, 55. The 18 connects Filton church and Westbury. The 20 connects Bishop Road/Kings Drive with Westbury. Services from Filton Church and St Werburgh's go directly to the city centre.*

Start from the side near Mogfords Ironmongers and go down the High Street away from the war memorial. There are toilets on the opposite side. Turn right into Church Road and walk towards Westbury Parish Church of The Holy Trinity.

Note the Elsie Briggs House of Prayer at the churchyard entrance on the right **A**. This, at over 600 years old, is the oldest house in Bristol. The oldest part of the church is the twelfth century north aisle and nave. It is open daily from 9.00am to 6.00pm.

Pass through the churchyard keeping the church on the left. Turn left down Chock Lane and then right into Trym Road. On your right note the culverted River Trym. Fork right by Dial House and go up the steps past the former Westbury Wildlife Park entrance.

The River Trym was navigable by ships up to 1099 when shifts in the land reduced it to a stream. Dial House **B** used to be a toll house for traffic crossing the river over a pack horse bridge.

Turn left at the top and then right into the alleyway in the far corner, passing through Cote Lea Park and Vintery Leys to reach Lakewood Road. Turn left and left again into Badocks Wood, following the footpath alongside a minor stream down to meet the River Trym again. Cross the footbridge and turn right to follow the Trym through and out of the woods up to Doncaster Road. Cross this road with care and continue to follow the Trym across Trowbridge Road to Shetland Road. Turn left, then right into Charfield Road, staying on the right-hand side of the road. Cross Pen Park Road via the zebra crossing and enter Stanton Road. Turn left into Fonthill Road and then right into Ascot Road. Go into the playground at the end of Ascot Road and follow the path ahead and then round to the left.

The tumuli-looking mounds dotted round the playground are only contractors' spoil heaps and are not significant. Note that the River Trym appears again by the fence on your right but is now reduced to a trickle in a ditch.

A short, heavily-wooded section lies ahead. Keeping the ditch to your right, carefully make your way through the wood following the ditch round to the left and up to the edge of the wood. Cross the ditch with care and pass onto Filton Golf Course. Turn left and keep to the edge of the wood as far as the footpath signpost pointing to the right.

Here is the source, sometimes scarcely damp, of the Westbury Trym, marked by a plain concrete block.

Take care of golfers while crossing the course, following the signpost direction towards another signpost by the perimeter fence of British Aerospace **C**.

The British and Colonial Aeroplane Company was founded in 1910 by Sir George White, owner of the Bristol Tramways Company, a concern known for its low wages, high fares and anti-union policy. It expanded during the war and changed its name to Bristol Aeroplane Company to avoid Excess Profits Duty. After that war it enjoyed Air Ministry support but failed to develop a civil market. Where other firms in the industry had to diversify widely into milk churns, fish friers, mushrooms or pianos, the Bristol Company, still a family firm, could make coach bodies for the tramways. In 1935, Bristol Aeroplane became a limited company, though the change was merely technical. Unlike domestic competitors it made both engines and airframes, not entirely to the satisfaction of the Ministry 'making useless and obsolete aircraft - many of which never left storage.' The aircraft side was a muddle without a marketing man and key items were imported. When war came the company was bailed out by the supply of American machine tools. After the war the firm ignored the jet. Eventually, the aircraft side was amalgamated with Vickers and English Electric in BAC. The engine division amalgamated with Armstrong Siddley and was absorbed by Rolls Royce.

Follow the footpath keeping close to the factory perimeter fence through the car park to reach Golf Course Lane. Cross over and turn right and follow the pavement round to the left all the way past The Mill House public house to the subway by the factory main entrance. (Note the statue of Pegasus on the seemingly derelict office building.) Take the subway under Gloucester Road North to Church Road where there are toilets and shops. Turn right back along Gloucester Road North towards Bristol as far as the roundabout and footbridge. Cross the footbridge into Filton Recreation Ground where there are seats for a flask coffee stop and/or rest.

Cross the recreation ground towards the far corner, bearing left to where Shellard Road meets Brabazon Road. Go down Brabazon Road a short distance and take the lane to the right between the playing field and garages. Follow this footpath, bearing left, until it reaches Filton Avenue. Take care crossing this road and go down the footpath opposite, turning right and then left, into Kipling Road. Cross over and follow the footpath opposite and go over the Temple Meads/ Parkway line railway bridge. Turn right and follow the footpath alongside the railway cutting, under the electricity power lines into a sports ground. Cross over the sports ground, heading towards the left hand side of the houses opposite and go through a gap in the railings.

Carry straight down a grassy space between buildings and through another gap in the railings. Turn right and follow the edge of the playing field round to the left into a short enclosed path into Landseer Avenue. Turn left and go up Hogarth Walk, past Lockleaze School. Turn right at the top and cross over the road.

Just past Lockleaze Adventure Playground, go through a kissing gate and enter Stoke Park. Follow the footpath round to the right and head towards a wide grassy corridor ahead, with the communications tower in the distance on your right. Shortly after the grassy corridor bends round to the right and the tower moves to your left, look out for a hedgerow coming in at right angles from the left. Cross through a gap in the hedge and go up the slope, keeping the hedgerow on your left and tower on your right hand. Pause at the top of the ridge to enjoy the stunning views all round here. Note the Dower House standing out on your left **D**.

Norborne Berkeley, later Lord Botetourt, rebuilt his family home in a gothic style. His sister, wife of the fourth Duke of Beaufort inherited it. Hence it came to be known as the Dower House, or 'the Duchess's'. In later years, it was a mental institution. The house is being refurbished and the immediate surroundings residentially developed.

Turn right along the ridge and pass through Purdown Camp **E**, *a World War II anti-aircraft gun battery site, and go past the communications tower* **F**. *Go down Sir John's Lane, named after one of the Smyth family who owned the land hereabouts, and turn left through the kissing gate at the bottom. Go down the lane and take the second turn right, after about 200 yards, opposite the first house and a door in the wall. Go down the field keeping the hedge to the right and enter the wood at the bottom. Go down the steps and onto Muller Road. Note the steps opposite. If there is little traffic, cross the road with care. Otherwise, go right down 200 yards to the pelican crossing and cross there. The 6 mile walk ends here. The bus routes pass Stottbury Road near the pelican crossing.*

Muller Road to Ashley Hill: return to and go up the steps, following the footpath round two sides of St Thomas More's School **G**. *Do not turn right in front of the school. Carry straight on down Allfoxton Road into Spalding Close.*

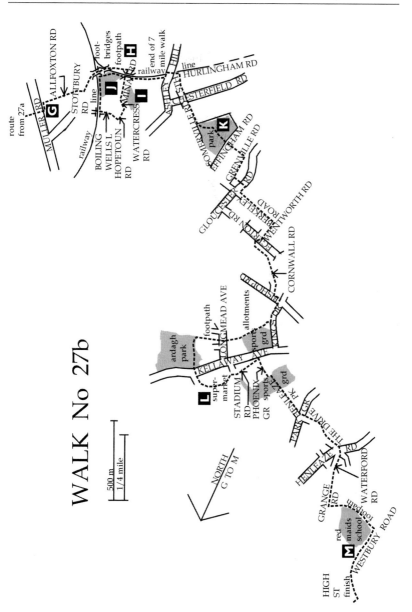

WALK No 27b

NORTH
G TO M

500 m
1/4 mile

Thomas More was born in 1478, wrote *Utopia* in 1516, was knighted by Henry VIII in 1521, and then beheaded by Henry in 1535 for refusing to take the oath of supremacy. He was finally canonised by Rome in 1935.

Go along the footpath at the end of Spalding Close and continue down to Narroways Junction where the Temple Meads to Severn Beach and Temple Meads to Parkway railway lines diverge. Cross over both railway bridges and descend past St Werburgh's Church .

This church formerly stood on the original cross-roads centre of Bristol (junction of Broad Street, Corn Street and High Street) but was removed to make way for road widening and rebuilt brick by brick in the 1870s. It is now a climbing centre.

Turn right into Mina Road. If you want to miss out the lunch stop section, take the footpath to the left before the railway bridge. This leads up to Ashley Hill, very close to where the recommended route ends. Otherwise, continue under the railway bridge and turn left into Watercress Road. A short distance up, opposite

St Werburgh City Farm ∎, *turn right into Hopetoun Road; the Farm is straight ahead. Note the café to the left of the pub which has some curiously decorated woodwork, of which more later.*

The route continues to a nearby picnic site known locally as The Top of The World. Go to the end of Hopetoun Road, turn right then left along Boiling Wells Lane as far as the Parkway line railway bridge.

Note the curiously decorated house back on the left, which was built by the same local builders who decorated the café beside the pub.

Go through the kissing gate and up the footpath to the right alongside the railway embankment. Turn right at the top into the Narroways Junction Millennium Green Nature Reserve where there is a large grassy area suitable for picnics ∎.

At Narroways junction, the branch line from Severn Beach joins the mainline to Cardiff. The branch line used to be directly linked to the Midland line to Bath via Mangotsfield. It is still possible to work out where the link left the branch line and crossed the GWR line here on its way to Kingswood junction.

Leave the picnic area by the surprisingly charming tree-lined level gravel footpath to the right, which runs alongside the Severn Beach railway line until the path turns right and passes through a kissing gate. Turn left to join another path which continues alongside the railway line as far as another kissing gate leading onto Ashley Hill. The 7 mile walk ends here. The bus route passes along Chesterfield Road a little further up the hill on the bend.

Ashley Hill to Westbury-on Trym: cross over Ashley Hill into Hurlingham Road. Turn right and go up Somerville Road South and then Somerville Road as far as St Andrew's Park ∎ *one of the largest and most popular neighbourhood parks with a fine bowling green, children's playground and toilets.*

The park is on the site of an old quarry. In 1882, the developer of St Andrew's offered the City twenty-two acres at a price the Corporation was unwilling to pay. Under pressure from local residents, the Corporation bought half the site in 1890 and for some years allowed its use as a tip, possibly to fill up the quarry, perhaps to raise revenue. Part of the park was laid out formally, part left for young people to amuse themselves. As usual, complaints followed attempted improvement. A plain park would have been preferable to a 'dressed up white elephant'. The bandstand, drinking fountain, railings, sundial and elaborate planting have gone, though some timber remains from the original conception and the lay-out of the walks survives.

Go into the park and leave by the bottom exit and cross Effingham Road into Grenville Road. Take the second turn right into North Road and, near the end, go down an alleyway on the left into Gloucester Road. There are toilets opposite. Cross the road, turn right and then left up Berkeley Road.

Take the second turn right into Wentworth Road and go though the alleyway at the end. Turn half left and go up Cornwall Road to Bishop Road. Turn left and then right into Kings Drive. Turn right into the lane on the left hand bend, then left and right to walk along a path between a sports ground and allotments. Continue on to Longmead Avenue. Cross over and enter the alley way opposite which leads into Ardagh Park Recreation Centre. This has tennis courts, a bowling green, attractive gardens and clubhouse. Turn left and go up past the children's playground to Kellaway Avenue. There are seats if a rest is needed. Use the controlled crossing lights to cross this busy road to the Tesco supermarket.

This supermarket was built on the Golden Hill sports ground after a lengthy protest. Nevertheless, it has a tea counter and toilets inside **L**.

Leave Tesco by the far end of the car park and turn left into Stadium Road. Turn right into Phoenix Grove and follow the footpath alongside Golden Hill Sports Ground. Go along Henleaze Park and down The Drive.

Cross over Henleaze Road and turn right along Waterford Road and Grange Park. Towards the end of Grange Park look out for the footpath on the left and follow it past Red Maids School into Westbury Road. Turn right down Westbury Hill.

Note the lock-up in the wall near the top of the hill just below and opposite the Post Office Tavern **M**.